Editor
Sara Connolly

Cover Artist
Tony Carrillo

Editor in Chief
Ina Massler Levin, M.A.

Creative Director
Karen J. Goldfluss, M.S. Ed.

Imaging
Ariyanna Simien

Publisher

Mary D. Smith, M.S. Ed.

Grades 4–8

Learn How To:

- create your own classroom blog
- create an interactive community
- share information immediately
- incorporate content and skills from academic areas

Teacher Created Resources

Author

Tracie Heskett, M.Ed.

Teacher Created Resources, Inc.
6421 Industry Way
Westminster, CA 92683
www.teachercreated.com

ISBN: 978-1-4206-2167-9

© 2009 Teacher Created Resources, Inc.
Made in U.S.A.

Table of Contents

Introduction

What Is a Blog?

A blog is a page on the Internet, a way to publish on the Web. Originally, the term "blog" referred to a web log, or a page on which people listed links to various websites and shared them with others, i.e., a log of places they visited on the Internet. The term "link" is short for "hyperlink," which is a way to connect one webpage with another page. When you click on the link it will redirect you to the linked section or page in the same website or another website. In other words, people would insert a link to another page on the Internet. If the reader clicked on the link, that page or website would open. Over time, people began to use blogs to write personal comments and reflections, and blogs became a form of online journaling. In this way, blogs provide a place for readers to write what they think about what they have read. Ideally, others will read the blog and comment with their reactions to the posted reflections, resulting in an ongoing conversation. Some people publish news and information on blogs that do not necessarily lend themselves to comments.

People also use blogs to list, or "log," their favorite blogs or websites of interest. Often a blog will focus on a particular topic or issue. Blogs may contain links to other websites, pictures, lists, videos, or other media content related to the topic. On the Internet, the blog displays the most recent entries first.

Blogs allow a group of people to communicate with each other on one or more specific topics. This format allows individuals to create their own publishing space with information, links, and ideas they want to keep for personal reference or to share with others.

Using This Book

The first section of this book introduces the vocabulary of blogs and programs, or platforms, that host blogs. It includes guidelines to help you plan and design one or more blogs to use with your students. Models of sample blogs illustrate various design elements. Throughout the text, pointers refer to sample lessons you may use with your students.

Three of the more common blog platforms are explained in subsequent sections. Each section contains guidelines for how to set up a blog, planning and customizing the blog, considerations for student use, and privacy and safety checklists. An overview of site navigation is also included.

You may use blogs from the sample blogs section on pages 62–65 in lessons or classroom discussions, or you can bookmark and display your favorite blogs as samples. A general overview of ways blogs can be used in the classroom is followed by specific sample lessons that will help you guide your students in learning how to use blogs in the classroom. The book concludes with an extensive list of Internet resources for teachers and students.

Why Use Blogs in the Classroom?

Initially, teachers used technology more in the classroom than the students did, for example—using SMART Boards™ or *Microsoft*® *PowerPoint*™ for classroom presentations. Students primarily used word processing programs, and perhaps the Internet for research, depending on availability of computers. Now students have greater access to the Internet, both in the classroom and outside of school.

Blogs offer an avenue for students to read new information and others' perspectives; they can interact and have discussions with other students, teachers, and potentially, others outside the immediate classroom community. Students may use blogs to respond to something they have read or new information they have learned. Students can gather information and research topics to share on the blog. Peers and others may respond to their comments, resulting in a conversation in which participants learn from each other.

✓ Sample Lesson: "Responding in Community," pages 72–73

> *"Blogs are a way to find out more about whatever topic the blog might be about. I want to know more about computers so I find a blog on that topic and subscribe to it. I might read what people have to say and then go read some new information about computers. Then I will post it on the blog, and see if people respond. Other people might not know what I found out so they might find that information valuable."*
>
> *–A.E., age 12*

As students post and comment on a blog, others read what they have written. Automatically, their writing has an authentic audience. Students respond to their peers' writing, evaluating and commenting on the writing.

Blogs enable you and your students to balance efficiency with self-directed learning. You can post announcements or interactive newsletters as well as assignments to reduce day-to-day accumulations of paper. A blog can point students to resources related to current topics of study and provide a way for students to make observations on content learning and participate in class discussion.

> *"[Blogs provide] …a different perspective on current events. … the traditional media [can be] very biased…"*
>
> *–J.S., parent*

Blogs work well for time-sensitive material, due to the immediacy of Internet communication. You can also post information you wish students to read. Students can post their work as requested or by choice. Student work may include assignments, personal reflections, opinions, and comments on material posted on the blog or outside information.

> *Many students already spend time online each day; they could take a few minutes to respond to questions posed by the teacher. Teachers could also post information and further questions not covered in class due to lack of time. Teachers can post homework assignments on a blog. It's faster to do homework on the computer and send it electronically. This eliminates student excuses, such as "I lost my paper," "the dog ate my paper," or "my printer broke."*
>
> *–B.W.M., age 19, teacher education student*

Why Use Blogs in the Classroom? *(cont.)*

You can configure a blog to set up individual student pages or small group pages to provide ways for students to interact, work collaboratively, and receive teacher feedback. All posts and comments have a date stamp which can help you ensure students participate as suggested.

Ideally, students might post or comment on a blog as a response to something they have read that interests them. The exercise of writing on a blog encourages students to think about and expand on their own ideas and thoughts about their culture and community. Students have the opportunity to interact with content material as well as other students' work. They use their background knowledge and preconceptions to respond to new ideas, comment on posts, and make connections with academic topics of current study.

> ✓ Sample Lesson: "Interact with Reading," pages 77–78

A classroom blog provides students with the opportunity to form an interactive community. The focus is on learning and sharing information, motivating students to discover the benefits of becoming lifelong learners. Students begin to realize that learning means letting go of old ideas, being willing to be wrong, and possibly change their thinking. Blogs also provide students with opportunities to become "experts" on a topic and share their knowledge with others. An interactive community develops as students read and then comment on what they have read. Not only do they comment on a post, but they read and comment on the comments pertaining to that post.

Blogs allow everyone to participate, regardless of ability. Quieter students may feel more comfortable communicating with peers via the written word. They have equal opportunity to express themselves, even with more vocal students in the group. Blogs offer one way to make thinking visible. Computers do not take into account how fast or slow students type; the information still gets transmitted. The more familiar students become with using technology to communicate in writing, the better they write.

You may also wish to list links on the class blogroll to specific blogs of interest. For example, students might read a blog about a topic of current study and engage in conversation about the author's thoughts, agreeing or disagreeing, and stating their reasons as they discuss what they read with their peers.

In summary, blogs offer students and teachers the following:

- regularly updated content
- unique style
- focused topics
- potential for immediate feedback
- an interactive community
- the ability to involve multiple people in an activity without complicated programming issues
- opportunities to write on specific themes
- a place to post rough drafts and receive feedback

Why Use Blogs in the Classroom? *(cont.)*

Making Time for Blogging

Academic standards and prescribed curriculum may leave you feeling you do not have time to add "one more thing" to your teaching day. As the sample lessons illustrate, working with blogs can incorporate content and skills from other academic subjects, such as reading, writing, science, and social studies. The following section on limited technology environments, along with the sample lessons, can give you ideas for teaching technology concepts within the framework of everyday classroom activities. Students may then apply the concepts of blogging outside the classroom within acceptable environments. In compliance with the Children's Online Privacy Protection Act, many blog platforms require children to be 13 or older to set up a blog. However, students may create a blog linked to a teacher's blog using Edublogs, perhaps during independent study time, or outside of school with another trusted family member setting up the blog. If you want to use the second option, you'll want to discuss it with parents and make blog set-up information and safety procedures available to them.

    ✓ Sample Lesson: "Blogging with Your Family," pages 79–80

Limited Technology Environments

You may need to take into consideration the availability of Internet access for students. One option for students who have limited access to the Internet is to have them write using a word processing program, then transfer their work to the class blog. Students may take turns entering their posts on classroom computers or computers in the computer lab or library. Alternatively, depending on students' computer abilities and classroom time constraints, volunteers could enter student information. This option removes students from active participation, however, and they become mostly readers rather than true contributors. If you do not have access to the Internet, many of the activities in the sample lessons section may be used to stimulate interactive conversations similar to a Web 2.0 environment using an overhead projector, chart paper, or a bulletin board. Regardless of the technology medium used, the goal is to have students read, respond, interact with content, and generate new content, rather than passively receive information from a teacher and restate facts on a test.

Blogs may be accessed via computers in a variety of locations. Students need not feel they have no access to the Internet. They can access a computer at school, in the public library, at an Internet café, at a friend or relative's house, or in their own homes.

Language Arts Standards: Reading

Level II (Grades 3–5)

Listed on pages 7–17 are McREL standards for Language Arts and Technology. All standards and benchmarks are used with permission from McREL.

Copyright 2009 McREL. Mid-continent Research for Education and Learning

Address: 4601 DTC Blvd, Suite 500, Denver, CO 80237. Telephone: (303) 337-0990

Website: www.mcrel.org/standards-benchmarks

Standard	Lesson	Pages
Standard 5. Uses the general skills and the strategies of the reading process		
Benchmark 2. Establishes a purpose for reading (e.g., for information, for pleasure, to understand a specific viewpoint	Responding in Community,	72–73
	Blogging with your Family,	79–80
	How to Respond on a Blog,	84–85
	On the Road to Responsible Blogging,	88–89
Benchmark 3. Makes, confirms, and revises simple predictions about what will be found in a text (e.g., uses prior knowledge, ideas presented in text, illustrations, graphic design, titles, topic sentences, key words, and foreshadowing clues	How to Post on a Blog	86–87
Benchmark 4. Uses phonetic and structural analysis techniques, syntactic structure, and semantic context to decode unknown words	Learning the Language	81–82
Benchmark 6. Uses word reference materials (e.g., glossary, dictionary, thesaurus) to determine the meaning, pronunciation, and derivations of unknown words	Learning the Language	81–82
Benchmark 7. Understands level-appropriate reading vocabulary (e.g., synonyms, antonyms, homophones, multi-meaning words)	How to Respond on a Blog	84–85

Language Arts Standards: Reading *(cont.)*

Level II (Grades 3–5) *(cont.)*

Standard	Lesson	Pages
Benchmark 8. Monitors own reading strategies and makes modifications as needed (e.g., recognizes when he or she is confused by a section of text, questions whether the text makes sense)	Blogging with Your Family	79–80
Standard 7. Uses reading skills and strategies to understand and interpret a variety of informational texts		
Benchmark 1. Uses reading skills and strategies to understand a variety of informational texts (e.g., biographical sketches, letters, diaries, Web pages)	Blogging with Your Family, How to Respond on a Blog, How to Post on a Blog	79–80 84–85 86–88
Benchmark 3. Uses text organizers (e.g., headings, topic and summary sentences, graphic features, typeface, chapter titles) to determine the main ideas and to locate information in a text	How to Post on a Blog	84–85
Benchmark 5. Summarizes and paraphrases information in texts (e.g., includes the main idea and significant supporting details of a reading selection)	Blogging with Your Family, How to Post on a Blog	79–80 86–87
Benchmark 6. Uses prior knowledge and experience to understand and respond to new information	Responding in Community, Blogging with Your Family, How to Post on a Blog	72–74 79–80 86–87
Benchmark 7. Understands structural patterns or organization in informational texts (e.g., chronological, logical, or sequential order; compare-and-contrast; cause-and-effect; proposition and support)	How to Respond on a Blog	84–85

Language Arts Standards: Reading *(cont.)*

Level III (Grades 6–8)

Standard	Lesson	Pages
Standard 5. Uses the general skills and the strategies of the reading process		
Benchmark 1. Establishes and adjusts purposes for reading (e.g., to understand, interpret, enjoy, solve problems, predict outcomes, answer a specific question, form an opinion, skim for facts; to discover models for own writing)	Responding in Community, Interact with Reading, How to Post on a Blog	72–73 77–78 86–87
Benchmark 2. Uses word origins and derivations to understand word meaning (e.g., Latin and Greek roots and affixes, meanings of foreign words frequently used in the English language, historical influences on English word meanings)	Learning the Language	81–82
Benchmark 3. Uses a variety of strategies to extend reading vocabulary (e.g., uses analogies, idioms, similes, metaphors to infer the meaning of literal and figurative phrases; uses definition, restatement, example, comparison and contrast to verify word meanings; identifies shades of meaning; knows denotative and connotative meanings; knows vocabulary related to different content areas and current events; uses rhyming dictionaries, classification books, etymological dictionaries)	Learning the Language	81–82
Benchmark 4. Uses specific strategies to clear up confusing parts of a text (e.g., pauses, rereads the text, consults another source, represents abstract information as mental pictures, draws upon background knowledge, asks for help)	Blogging with Your Family, On the Road to Responsible Blogging	79–80 88–89
Benchmark 6. Reflects on what has been learned after reading and formulates ideas, opinions, and personal responses to texts	Blogging with Your Family, How to Respond on a Blog, How to Post on a Blog	79–80 84–85 86–87
Benchmark 6. Reflects on what has been learned after reading and formulates ideas, opinions, and personal responses to texts	Interact with Reading, Blogging with Your Family	77–78 79–80

Language Arts Standards: Reading (cont.)

Level III (Grades 6–8) (cont.)

Standard	Lesson	Pages
Standard 7. Uses reading skills and strategies to understand and interpret a variety of informational texts		
Benchmark 1. Uses reading skills and strategies to understand a variety of informational texts (e.g., electronic texts; textbooks; biographical sketches; directions; essays; primary source historical documents, including letters and diaries; print media, including editorials, news stories, periodicals, and magazines; consumer, workplace, and public documents, including catalogs, technical directions, procedures, and bus routes)	Blogging with Your Family, How to Respond on a Blog, How to Post on a Blog	79–80 84–85 86–87
Benchmark 2. Knows the defining characteristics of a variety of informational texts (e.g., electronic texts; textbooks; biographical sketches; letters; diaries; directions; procedures; magazines; essays; primary source historical documents; editorials; news stories; periodicals; bus routes; catalogs; technical directions; consumer, workplace, and public documents)	On the Road to Responsible Blogging	88–89
Benchmark 3. Summarizes and paraphrases information in texts (e.g., arranges information in chronological, logical, or sequential order; conveys main ideas, critical details, and underlying meaning; uses own words or quoted materials; preserves author's perspective and voice)	Blogging with your Family	79–80
Benchmark 4. Uses new information to adjust and extend personal knowledge base	Responding in Community, Learning the Language, How to Post on a Blog	72–73 81–82 86–87
Benchmark 5. Draws conclusions and makes inferences based on explicit and implicit information in texts	Responding in Community, How to Respond on a Blog, How to Post on a Blog	72–73 84–85 86–87
Benchmark 6. Differentiates between fact and opinion in informational texts	How to Respond on a Blog	84–85

Language Arts Standards: Writing

Level II (Grades 3–5)

Standard	Lesson	Pages
Standard 1. Uses the general skills and the strategies of the writing process		
Benchmark 1. Prewriting: Uses prewriting strategies to plan written work (e.g., uses graphic organizers, story maps, and webs; groups related ideas; takes notes; brainstorms ideas; organizes information according to type and purpose of writing)	Blogging with Your Family, How to Post on a Blog	79–80 86–87
Benchmark 2. Drafting and Revising: Uses strategies to draft and revise written work (e.g., elaborates on a central idea; writes with attention to audience, word choice, and sentence variation; uses paragraphs to develop separate ideas; produces multiple drafts)	Designing a Blog, How to Post on a Blog	83 86–87
Benchmark 3. Editing and Publishing: Uses strategies to edit and publish written work (e.g., edits for grammar, punctuation, capitalization, and spelling at a developmentally appropriate level; uses reference materials; considers page format, e.g., paragraphs, margins, indentations, titles; selects presentation format according to purpose; incorporates photos, illustrations, charts, and graphs; uses available technology to compose and publish work)	Blogging with Your Family, Learning the Language, How to Post on a Blog	79–80 81–82 86–87
Benchmark 4. Evaluates own and others' writing (e.g., determines the best features of a piece of writing, determines how own writing achieves its purposes, asks for feedback, responds to classmates' writing)	Designing a Blog, How to Respond on a Blog	83 84–85
Benchmark 6. Writes for a variety of purposes (e.g., adapts focus, point of view, organization, form; writes to inform, entertain, explain, describe, record ideas)	Responding in Community, Interact with Reading, Blogging with Your Family, Learning the Language, How to Post on a Blog, On the Road to Responsible Blogging	72–73 77–78 79–80 81–82 86–87 88–89

Language Arts Standards: Writing *(cont.)*

Level II (Grades 3–5) *(cont.)*

Standard	Lesson	Pages
Benchmark 7. Writes expository compositions (e.g., identifies and stays on the topic; develops the topic with simple facts, details, examples, and explanations; excludes extraneous and inappropriate information; uses structures such as cause-and-effect, chronology, similarities and differences; uses several sources of information; provides a concluding statement)	How to Post on a Blog	86–87
Benchmark 10. Writes expressive compositions (e.g., expresses ideas, reflections, and observations; uses an individual, authentic voice; uses narrative strategies, relevant details, and ideas that enable the reader to imagine the world of the event of experience)	Responding in Community, Interact with Reading, How to Respond on a Blog	72–73 77–78 84–85
Benchmark 11. Writes in response to literature (e.g., summarizes main ideas and significant details; relates own ideas to supporting details; advances judgments; supports judgments with references to the text, other works, other authors, nonprint media, and personal knowledge)	Responding in Community, Interact with Reading, How to Respond on a Blog	72–73 77–78 84–85
Benchmark 12. Writes personal letters (e.g., includes the date, address, greeting, body, and closing; addresses envelopes; includes signature)	How to Respond on a Blog	84–85
Standard 2. Uses the stylistic and rhetorical aspects of writing		
Benchmark 1. Uses descriptive language that clarifies and enhances ideas (e.g., common figures of speech, sensory details)	Blogging with Your Family, Designing a Blog, How to Post on a Blog	79–80 83 86–87

Language Arts Standards: Writing (cont.)

Level II (Grades 3–5) (cont.)

Standard	Lesson	Pages
Benchmark 2. Uses paragraph form in writing (e.g., indents the first word of a paragraph, uses topic sentences, recognizes a paragraph as a group of sentences about one main idea, uses an introductory and concluding paragraph, writes several related paragraphs)	Blogging with Your Family, Designing a Blog, How to Post on a Blog	79–80 83 86–87
Benchmark 3. Uses a variety of sentence structures in writing (e.g., expands basic sentence patterns, uses exclamatory or imperative sentences	Blogging with Your Family, Designing a Blog, How to Post on a Blog	79–80 83 86–87
Standard 4. Gathers and uses information for research purposes		
Benchmark 3. Uses dictionaries to gather information for research topics	Learning the Language	81–82
Benchmark 5. Uses key words, guide words, alphabetical and numerical order, indexes, cross-references, and letters on volumes to find information for research topics	Learning the Language	81–82
Benchmark 7. Uses strategies to gather and record information for research topics (e.g., uses notes, maps, charts, graphs, tables, and other graphic organizers; paraphrases and summarizes information; gathers direct quotes; provides narrative description)	Blogging with Your Family	79–80
Benchmark 8. Uses strategies to compile information into written reports or summaries (e.g., incorporates notes into a finished product; includes simple facts, details, explanations, and examples; draws conclusions from relationships and patterns that emerge from data from different sources; uses appropriate visual aids and media)	Blogging with Your Family, Learning the Language	79–80 81–82
Benchmark 9. Cites information sources (quotes or paraphrases information sources, lists resources used by title)	Blogging with Your Family	79–80

Language Arts Standards: Writing *(cont.)*

Level III (Grades 6–8)

Standard	Lesson	Pages
Standard 1. Uses the general skills and strategies of the writing process		
Benchmark 2. Drafting and Revising: Uses a variety of strategies to draft and revise written work (e.g., analyzes and clarifies meaning, makes structural and syntactical changes, uses an organizational scheme, uses sensory words and figurative language, rethinks and rewrites for different audiences and purposes, checks for a consistent point of view and for transitions between paragraphs, uses direct feedback to revise compositions)	Learning the Language, Designing a Blog	81–82 83
Benchmark 4. Evaluates own and others' writing (e.g., applies criteria generated by self and others, uses self-assessment to set and achieve goals as a writer, participates in peer response groups)	Designing a Blog	83
Benchmark 5. Writes for specific audiences (e.g., public, private) and uses appropriate content, style, and structure (e.g., formal or informal language, genre, organization)	Blogging with Your Family, How to Post on a Blog	79–80 86–87
Benchmark 6. Writes for specific purposes (e.g., to entertain, to influence, to inform)	Blogging with Your Family	79–80
Benchmark 7. Writes expository compositions (e.g., states a thesis or purpose, presents information that reflects knowledge about the topic of the report, organizes and presents information in a logical manner, including an introduction and conclusion, uses own words to develop ideas, uses common expository structures and features, such as compare-contrast or problem-solution)	Designing a Blog	83
Benchmark 11. Writes persuasive compositions (e.g., engages the reader by establishing a context, creating a persona, and otherwise developing reader interest; develops a controlling idea that conveys a judgment; creates and organizes a structure appropriate to the needs and interests of a specific audience; arranges details, reasons, examples, and/or anecdotes persuasively; excludes information and arguments that are irrelevant; anticipates and addresses reader concerns and counter arguments; supports arguments with detailed evidence, citing sources of information as appropriate)	Responding in Community	72–73
Benchmark 12. Writes compositions that address problems/ solutions (e.g., identifies and defines a problem in a way appropriate to the intended audience, describes at least one solution, presents logical and well-supported reasons)	On the Road to Responsible Blogging	88–89

Language Arts Standards: Writing (cont.)

Level III (Grades 6–8) *(cont.)*

Standard	Lesson	Pages
Benchmark 13. Writes in response to literature (e.g., responds to significant issues in a log or journal; answers discussion questions; anticipates and answers a reader's questions; writes a summary of a book; describes an initial impression of a text; connects knowledge from a text with personal knowledge; states an interpretive, evaluative, or reflective position; draws inferences about the effects of the work on an audience)	Responding in Community, How to Respond on a Blog	72–73 84–85
Benchmark 15. Writes technical text, such as bylaws for an organization (e.g., identifies essential steps in a logical sequence, lists materials or equipment needed, describes all factors and variables that need to be considered, uses appropriate formatting)	Blogging with Your Family, Learning the Language	79–80 81–82
Standard 2. Uses the stylistic and rhetorical aspects of writing		
Benchmark 1. Uses descriptive language that clarifies and enhances ideas (e.g., establishes time and mood, uses figurative language, uses sensory images and comparisons, uses a thesaurus to choose effective wording)	Blogging with Your Family, Designing a Blog, How to Post on a Blog	79–80 83 86–87
Benchmark 2. Uses paragraph form in writing (e.g., arranges sentences in sequential order, uses supporting and follow-up sentences, establishes coherence within and among paragraphs)	Blogging with Your Family, Designing a Blog, How to Post on a Blog	79–80 83 86–87
Benchmark 3. Uses a variety of sentence structures to expand and embed ideas (e.g., simple, compound, and complex sentences; parallel structure, such as similar grammatical forms or juxtaposed items)	Blogging with Your Family, Designing a Blog, How to Post on a Blog	79–80 83 86–87
Benchmark 4. Uses explicit transitional devices	Blogging with Your Family	79–80

Technology Standards

Level II (Grades 3–5)

Standard	Lesson	Pages
Standard 2. Knows the characteristics and uses of computer software programs		
Benchmark 1. Uses a word processor to edit, copy, move, save, and print text with some formatting (e.g., centering lines, using tabs, forming paragraphs)	Learning the Language, How to Post on a Blog	81–82 86–87
Standard 4. Understands the nature of technological design		
Benchmark 3. Knows that the design process is a series of methodical steps for turning ideas into useful products and systems	Designing a Blog	83
Benchmark 7. Evaluates a product or design (e.g., considers how well the product or design met the challenge to solve a problem; considers the ability of the product or design to meet constraints), and makes modifications based on results	Designing a Blog	83
Standard 5. Understands the nature and operation of systems		
Benchmark 1. Knows that when things are made up of many parts, the parts usually affect one another	Responding in Community, Blogging with Your Family	72–73 79–80
Benchmark 3. Understands the relationships between elements (i.e., components, such as people or parts) in systems	Responding in Community	72–73

Technology Standards (cont.)

Level III (Grades 6–8)

Standard	Lesson	Pages
Standard 2. Knows the characteristics and uses of computer software programs		
Benchmark 1. Uses advanced features and utilities of word processors (e.g., uses clip art, a spell-checker, grammar checker, thesaurus, outliner)	Learning the Language	81–82
Benchmark 2. Knows the common features and uses of desktop publishing software (e.g., documents are created, designed, and formatted for publication; data, graphics, and scanned images can be imported into a document using desktop software)	Learning the Language	81–82
Standard 4. Understands the nature of technological design		
Benchmark 2. Knows that the design process relies on different strategies: creative brainstorming to establish many design solutions, evaluating the feasibility of various solutions in order to choose a design, and troubleshooting the selected design	Designing a Blog	83
Benchmark 6. Evaluates the ability of a technological design to meet criteria established in the original purpose (e.g., considers factors that might affect acceptability and suitability for intended users or beneficiaries; develop measures of quality with respect to these factors), suggests improvements, and tries proposed modifications	Designing a Blog	83

ISTE NETS for Teachers

International Society for Technology in Education
National Educational Technology Standards

(working document—Copyright ISTE 2008)

Standard	Lesson	Pages
Standard 1. Facilitate and Inspire Student Learning and Creativity Teachers use their knowledge of teaching, learning, and technology to facilitate learning experiences that advance student creativity and innovation in both face-to-face and virtual environments. Teachers:		
A. promote, support, and model creative and innovative thinking and inventiveness	Designing a Blog, How to Respond on a Blog, How to Post on a Blog	83 84–85 86–87
C. promote student reflection using collaborative tools to illuminate their own thinking, planning, and creative processes	Responding in Community, Blogging with Your Family, Designing a Blog, How to Respond on a Blog	72–73 79–80 83 84–85
D. model knowledge construction and creative thinking by engaging in face-to-face and virtual learning with students, colleagues, and others	How to Respond on a Blog, How to Post on a Blog, On the Road to Responsible Blogging	84–85 86–87 88–89
Standard 2. Design Digital-Age Learning Experiences and Assessments Teachers plan and design authentic learning experiences and assessments incorporating contemporary tools and resources to maximize content learning in context and to develop the knowledge, skills, and attitudes identified in the NETS. Teachers:		

ISTE NETS for Teachers *(cont.)*

ISTE NETS for Teachers *(cont.)*

Standard	Lesson	Pages
A. design or adapt relevant learning experiences to incorporate digital tools and resources that promote student learning and creativity	Interact with Reading, Learning the Language, How to Respond on a Blog	77–78 81–82 84–85
B. develop technology-enriched learning environments that enable students to become active participants in setting their own educational goals, managing their own learning, and assessing their own progress	How to Post on a Blog	86–87
Standard 3. Model Digital-Age Work and Learning Teachers exhibit knowledge, skills, and work processes that are representative of an innovative professional in a global and digital society. Teachers:		
B. collaborate with students, peers, parents, and community members using digital tools and resources to support student success and innovation	How to Post on a Blog	86–87
C. communicate relevant information and ideas effectively to students, parents, and peers using a variety of digital-age media and formats	Blogging with Your Family, How to Post on a Blog, On the Road to Responsible Blogging	79–80 86–87 88–89
D. model and facilitate effective use of current and emerging digital tools to locate, analyze, evaluate, and use information resources to support research and learning	Blogging with Your Family, Learning the Language, How to Post on a Blog	79–80 86–87 86–87
Standard 4. Promote Digital Citizenship and Responsibility Teachers understand local and global societal issues and responsibilities in an evolving digital culture and exhibit legal and ethical behavior in their professional practices. Teachers:		
A. advocate, model, and teach safe, legal, and ethical use of digital information and technology, including respect of copyright and the appropriate documentation of sources	Blogging with Your Family, On the Road to Responsible Blogging	79–80 88–89
C. promote digital etiquette and responsible social interactions related to the use of technology and information	Blogging with Your Family, How to Post on a Blog, On the Road to Responsible Blogging	79–80 86–87 88–89

Learning about Blogs

District Internet Safety Procedures

Before beginning any blog project, inform appropriate administrative personnel and become familiar with district technology policies, Internet acceptable use procedures (AUP), firewalls, etc. that are currently in place. Check to ensure the district firewall allows traffic to and from the selected blog platform. Obtain parent/guardian permission in accordance with district policies for students' participation in online/Internet activities. Consider having students sign a permission form or an acceptable use policy that includes statements of who can post and who can comment, or a statement indicating they understand the classroom rules and terms of use for participating in the blog community.

✓ Sample: "Student Internet Agreement," page 66

✓ Sample: "Parent/Guardian Permission Form," page 67

Blog Terminology

administrator	someone who has authority to change blog settings
archive	a collection of all your posts on one page; may be organized by date or category
author	someone who writes posts to a blog
avatar	a two-dimensional picture used on the Internet to represent a computer user
blog	a page on the Internet that can be public or private
blogosphere	the Internet blogging community
blogroll	a list of links to sites you want to share
category	a broad grouping of post topics
comment	a reader's response to a post, or an original message
contributor	someone who can write posts to a blog; administrator must approve posts
dashboard	a user interface that organizes and presents information in a way that is easy to read
domain	an Internet address owned by a company, organization, or individual
editor	someone who can edit posts and comments, and has the ability to delete
forum	an online discussion group
IP address	an identifier for a computer on a network
moderate (comments)	to decide whether or not posts are appropriate for the blog
password	a secret series of letters and numbers that allows a user to access a file, web page, blog, computer, or program

Learning about Blogs *(cont.)*

Blog Terminology *(cont.)*

ping	helps notify other blog-tracking tools of updates, changes, and trackbacks; a utility to determine whether or not a specific IP address is accessible
blog platform	a computer program or service that hosts blogs
post	original messages placed on a blog, published entries
reader	a list of favorite sites and new posts on those sites, using programs such as **www.google.com/reader** or **www.bloglines.com**
RSS feeds	new posts on other blogs feed into your reader
subscriber	someone who reads a blog; or, someone who subscribes to a blog via RSS feeds
tag	a label or keyword associated with individual posts in a blog that describes the post in more detail
trackbacks	when someone writes about a post on another blog and includes a link to that other blog; a ping is sent to another blog to notify them that their article has been mentioned by you
traffic	the measure of the number of visitors who visit a blog
URL	the address of a website on the World Wide Web
user name	the name a person uses for the blog
widgets	"A widget is a self-contained piece of code that you can move into, out of, and anywhere inside the sidebar area of your blog." (**http://faq.wordpress.com/2006/12/24/what-is-a-widget/**)
WYSIWYG	"What you see is what you get" which means that the way something appears on your screen is the way it will appear on the web.

✓ Sample Lesson: "Learning the Language," pages 81–82

Blog Platforms

This book focuses on two or three common blog platforms that lend themselves well to classroom use and are easy to access and set up.

Blogger

http://www.blogger.com

Many people have seen blogs hosted by Blogger.com. Blogger allows comment moderation and restriction of authors of new posts, as well as the option to limit who may read and comment on the blog. There is some concern about the "navigation bar" in Blogger, which allows readers to link to other (unknown) sites. This function may be turned off, which also limits the blog's exposure on the Internet. The blog administrator may set reader settings separate from author settings. More than one blog administrator may be specified. It is easy to use Blogger and add page elements to a blog. Page elements that may be added include but are not limited to: links to other webpages, pictures, lists, or a visitor counter, which can be added with external code.

Edublogs

http://www.edublogs.org

Edublogs.org has many of same features as Blogger. It allows the user to create one or more web pages linked to the blog. Edublogs offers a "free WordPress-powered blog." The site also offers many documents and tips to help teachers use blogs in the classroom with their students. At times this site loads and navigates very slowly.

WordPress

http://www.wordpress.com

Wordpress is the host company that Edublogs uses. It has many of the same features but appears to load and navigate faster than Edublogs. WordPress offers a blog tracker that allows teachers to easily track traffic on the blog. You may use some of the disclaimer verbiage from the site to create your own terms and conditions for your blogs, as long as you give WordPress credit.

However, WordPress does not offer the Blog & User Creator feature that allows you to create student blogs linked to a main classroom blog. It has more available widgets for the side bar. Users may choose from a variety of themes; some have options to customize header and blog colors. Different themes offer different features, such as number of columns of text, variations on width, and the ability to create parent pages.

Other blog platform options include Think.com, Typepad (a paid host), Yahoo! 360° (similar to My Space), 21classes, and Livejournal.com. Class Blogmeister focuses exclusively on education and requires a school pass code to register. Moodle can be set up to offer forums for students to use to connect with teachers.

Planning a Blog

∽∽∽

Once you determine you would like to use one or more blogs in your classroom, you will need to consider which blog platform would be best to use. In the initial planning stages, ask questions about how you plan to use the blog in your classroom, including the tasks you expect students to complete on the blog. In general, you will need to establish instructional goals (teacher-generated) as well as community (student-generated) goals for the blog(s).

Questions to ask:

✓ What is the general purpose of the blog?

✓ What are my instructional goals for the blog(s)?

✓ What goals do the students have as a classroom community for the blog(s)?

✓ What do I want students to gain from the experience?

✓ Do students have enough keyboarding (typing) skills to be able to successfully write and post entries on a blog? If not, how can they learn those skills? Or, how can their work get posted to the blog?

✓ How often and how much content do I expect students to post? Do I want a formal schedule to track students' posting?

✓ Do I want readers outside the classroom to be able to read the blog?

✓ Who do I want to comment on the blog? Anyone or only registered users?

✓ Do I want to be able to moderate comments before they post to the blog?

✓ Who do I want to allow to post (contribute) to the blog?

✓ Will students have their own blogs that they can use as a portfolio for their work? If so, how will other class members access them to make comments on student work?

✓ What page elements do I want to include?

✓ Which blog platform will best suit these purposes?

✓ Will I grade student work posted online? If so, how?

If a school or district has firewalls or other restrictions on Internet use, that may also affect the choice of setup for a blog. The blog platforms suggested in this book should be accessible through any computer that has access to the Internet.

✓ Sample: "Parent/Guardian Permission Form," pages 67–68

You may also wish to gather student information prior to setting up a classroom blog, particularly if student blogs will be linked to the classroom blog home page. "Student Blog Input," page 31, or "Planning My Blog," page 39, will assist you in gathering this information. Enlist a volunteer if possible to do the actual input, for example, a parent or other classroom aide. Older students may enter their own information depending on the amount of Internet experience they have had in the classroom.

Designing the Blog

The key factors to consider when designing a blog are theme (message) and audience. Members of the classroom community (teacher and students) should think about specific topics they might address on the blog, what they want to say, and who will be interested in reading their blog. Several other factors also contribute to the design of a blog. Effective blogs have various features, including:

- **author biography**—This is the "about us" page. You need not display specific student names; a paragraph about grade level, region of the country, purpose in creating the blog, any expertise about a particular topic, or other motivation behind the project will suffice.

- **photos**—Check district guidelines before posting any pictures containing student images, even group pictures. Students may post pictures of their work, projects, or classroom displays.

- **descriptive headlines**—Readers search based on key words in the titles of blogs or posts on blogs. This provides great opportunities for students to practice writing leads that catch the reader's attention.

- **links**—Clearly state where links lead. Identify links with colored, underlined text. Do not underline other text in the blog.

- **categories**—These help readers navigate through specific topics on the blog.

Blogs may have one, two, or three columns to display information. Some templates allow users to change font colors, customize the header, or move page elements around. Aside from the blog's appearance, consider also accessing control settings, password options, and linked pages.

Involve students in the process of designing the blog(s) for the classroom. Conduct a class discussion on what to name the blog, how to describe the blog, what image(s) to include in the header or as page elements on the blog, and font style and color.

✓ Sample Lesson: "Designing a Blog," page 83

Managing Blogs

Blog platforms offer various tools to help contributors organize and find posts and other information on the blog. Each blog entry may have a category, or a label that identifies a general post topic. Posts may also have tags, which provide a more specific way to classify, or sort, blog entries.

Tips and Cautions

- Set the teacher as the only administrator.

- Have students use user names or an alpha-numeric system with initials and numbers to protect privacy.

- Keep a written log of any and all usernames, passwords, blog domains (URLs), and any other information pertinent to any blogs you set up.

- Have clear expectations, rules, and consequences.

- Remind students to always leave "remember me" boxes unchecked for automatic password retrieval.

- Whenever the Internet browser asks if it should remember this password, click "no."

- Consider setting up students' user names as categories.

- Students should plan any blog or other web page *prior* to building it.

- Consider setting a password to publish—to which only the teacher has access. The teacher then approves all posts before publishing on the Internet.

- Use RSS feed aggregator to subscribe to student web pages.

- You might want to add a page element (sidebar or box) listing the most pertinent posts so those posts do not get buried in archives.

- If the class has access to a domain and web page, the blog can be part of the class web page.

- Students set to "editor" role can edit teacher's posts. They can also edit other students' pages. (See "Student Internet Agreement," page 66.) However, students set to "author" role cannot write pages at all. You would have to set up individual student pages and move appropriate posts.

- Students can change their own profile (email and password) regardless of role without notification to administrator (teacher); incorporate wording in the user agreement students will sign that states they agree not to change their email or password.

- Teachers cannot access student profiles.

- If students will be set up as editor, also put in the student agreement that they will not delete administrator posts.

Managing Blogs *(cont.)*

Tips and Cautions *(cont.)*

- Encourage students to post only original material, no copyrighted material.

- Remind students to post only appropriate information.

- Remind students that they never know who might read a post—they should only write information they would be willing for the world—that includes anyone they know (friend or enemy), parents, teachers, etc., to read.

- "Net-etiquette" says that many people view all caps as shouting; it is also harder to read.

- Some educators feel that if students are assigned to "blog," the requirement detracts from the original purpose and spirit of blogging.

    ✓ Sample: "Student Internet Agreement," page 66

Writing Blog Content—Posts and Comments

Effective blogs—those that attract readers and comments—share many common characteristics. Contributors to a blog create quality content when they write posts that are useful and unique. At the outset, you and your students will want to identify your intended audience and ask yourselves what those people will want to read. Effective blogs have regular posts and focused content. A blog may have one of several purposes as it seeks to catch and hold readers' attention. Some reasons for writing on a blog include

- entertainment—for fun

- education—the reader will learn more about a topic

- information—giving readers information about issues, products, or specific topics

- debate or dialogue—to discuss certain issues or topics

- news—to keep readers up-to-date on current events

- community—to encourage people to connect and interact with one another

When posting and commenting on a blog, students need to remember the obvious: they are writing material that will be published online, rather than in print. This fact has implications that affect how user friendly a blog is for the reader. The appearance and layout of text makes the content easier or more difficult to read.

You may want to look at the sample blogs on pages 62–65 as you think about the purpose(s) of your blog.

Managing Blogs *(cont.)*

Text Considerations

- ❏ font size
- ❏ font color contrast with background
- ❏ underline only text links
- ❏ break up large blocks of text
  - subheads
  - bulleted lists
  - highlight key words
  - short paragraphs
- ❏ present information using the inverted pyramid (most important details first)
- ❏ use a simple writing style
- ❏ use simple language

What happens when technology fails?

In the event the blog "crashes" or is accidentally deleted, keep copies of significant posts or thread topics in a simple word processing file. Posts can easily be copied and pasted from the Internet into the word processing file. A separate file—hard copy or stored offline in another computer document—should also be maintained with passwords and user names. If the Internet connection is down for a period of time and you wish to keep the interactive conversation of the blog going, refer to the sample lesson on pages 72–73 to continue a "paper-and-pencil" blog. Many of the other sample lessons may also be taught offline. Or, have a back-up lesson plan that requires no technology.

It is also possible to save the word processing files to a flash drive and maintain the interactive community on another computer system.

Edublogs

http://www.edublogs.org

This blog platform targets educators and students. The site provides a valuable support forum with information on how to use blogs with students in the classroom. Take some time to investigate their home website and read the tips from other teachers.

Edublogs allows the administrator to load an entire contact address list from a web-based email service, such as Hotmail or Yahoo!, which makes creating a community list of users fairly easy. The administrator may also add users individually. Users may be listed as subscribers, contributors, authors, or editors. Keep administrative authority so you can maintain access to the blog and make changes to blog settings as necessary; do not set student users to administrator.

Getting Started

To sign up as a new user on Edublogs:

1. Go to **http://www.edublogs.org**. Click on the link to **Sign Up Here**. This page will direct you to create a username, at least four characters, numbers and lowercase letters only. Your user name will appear on your dashboard and as you navigate around the site whenever you are logged in to edublogs. This user name will be linked to the email address you enter. You may have more than one blog under this account. For each separate blog, you will use this same user name to log in. If you want to set up a separate account with a different user name, you must use a different email address.

2. Enter your email address.

3. Read the terms of service and check the box beside "I agree:" stating that you are involved in education.

4. Enter the verification code if shown.

5. Check one of the two boxes:

   "Gimme a blog!" or

   "Just a username, please"

6. Click on **Next**.

   A. The first option, "Gimme a blog!," directs the user to the next page.

      1. This page assigns the blog a domain, which will become your URL, or Internet address, e.g., "ClassroomofLearners.edublogs.org."

      2. You will then write a blog title, or what you want to name your blog, e.g., "Classroom of Learners."

      3. Check your preferred privacy settings for the blog.

      4. Enter the type of blog: teacher, student, or other.

      5. Select language, and click on **Signup**.

Getting Started *(cont.)*

Edublogs will then direct you to a new screen.

1. This screen will list your blog title. The site requests that you activate the blog.

2. Check your email at the address you provided and open the message from edublogs.org, then click on the link given.

3. You will see a pop-up window screen from Edublogs with your username and password. When you first set up a username, Edublogs will assign a random (letters and numbers) password and you will also receive an email. Once you log in to the blog's home page, you can go to a link that will allow you to change the password.

4. Note the user name and random password in a safe place.

B. The second option, "Just a username," directs the user to a new page. (See page 32 for further explaination of the "Just a username" option.)

1. This page shows the full **User Name** entered on the previous screen.

2. The site directs the user to activate the blog.

3. Check your email at the address you provided on the previous screen and open the message sent from Edublogs.org, then click on the link given.

4. You will see a pop-up window screen from Edublogs with your username and password. When you first set up a username, Edublogs will assign a random (letters and numbers) password and you will also receive an email. Once you log in to the blog's home page, you can go to a link that will allow you to change the password.

5. Note the user name and random password in a safe place.

Once you have an account set up with Edublogs, you may choose from one of several options to add students to a class blog.

For younger students or to keep classroom blog activities separate from students' personal email, use the filter option in Gmail to link students to a central (teacher) email account.

✓ Sign in to Gmail with your main email address and password.

✓ At the top of the main Gmail page is a link to **create a filter**.

✓ Click on the link. The site will redirect to a page subtitled "Create a Filter."

✓ In the box **To:** type in "[your gmail address]+[student name or user name]@gmail.com"

✓ Click on **Next Step**.

✓ On the next page, check the box **Apply the label**.

✓ Use the arrow key to open the window. Select "New label."

✓ In the window, type the student name or user name to match the filter entered on the previous screen.

✓ Click **OK**.

Getting Started *(cont.)*

Email generated by the blog will all go to this one central account. To set up students on the **Blog & User Creator** page you will still need to enter each student individually, but the email addresses will be similar and easy to remember.

You may wish to conduct a lesson/class activity to help students generate and compile the information that will be needed to set up student blogs. Have students use the "Student Blog Input" form on page 31 to create a user name, preferred email address (for older students setting up their own Gmail accounts), a title for their blog, and a password that will be easy for them to remember. Student user names may be a combination of their initials, numbers, or some other code that will be easy for students and teacher to recognize within the classroom, but do not use the students' real names if the blog will be visible to readers outside the immediate classroom environment. Encourage students to create a password that is about eight characters in length, with a combination of letters and numbers. Use the student user name as part of the URL. You may want to use the last column, "Design Choice," only with older students. Once student blogs have been set up, log in as administrator and complete the following tasks:

✓ select the design (template) for the blog

✓ set discussion and privacy settings

✓ confirm blog type as "student"

✓ add other classmates to student's blog if they will do anything other than comment on peer's blogs

✓ change avatar if desired (this would take a lot of time!)

Student Blog Input

Student Name	User Name	User Email	Blog Title	Blog URL	User Password	Design choice
Elsie	*elrose*	*elsiefx2@gmail.com*	*Elrose Explorers*	*elrose.edublogs.org*	*integrity99*	

Student Blogging

Option #1

One class blog, administered by teacher

- Go to main teacher Gmail account.

- Create filters and labels for students.

- Sign out of any open Edublog accounts.

- Go to **www.edublogs.org**.

- Click on **Sign up for free**.

- Sign up for "Gimme a blog!" if you have not already created the class blog; otherwise sign up for "Just a username, please."

- Complete the "Getting Started" steps on page 28 and 29.

- Go back to **www.edublogs.org**.

- Sign in with your user name and password.

- Go to **Users** tab **Add Users** to add students.

- Use the "teacheremail+student" gmail address.

- Set student roles (see "Student User Roles" chart, pages 35–37).

- Students may comment on your posts and start new discussions by making their own posts, depending on their user role.

Sample #1: Class blog

http://lizardgirl.edublogs.org/

- The teacher is the only administrator

- Students comment as authors

- Teacher typically posts questions

- Students reply to questions, which may require research

Option #2

One class blog, administered by teacher; students have individual pages

- Go to main teacher Gmail account.

- Create filters and labels for students.

- Sign out of any open Edublog accounts.

- Go to **www.edublogs.org**.

- Click on **Sign up for free**.

- Sign up for "Gimme a blog!"

- Go back to **www.edublogs.org**.

Student Blogging *(cont.)*

Option #2 *(cont.)*

- Sign in with your user name and password.

- Begin as in Option #1.

- Go to **Users** tab **Add Users** to add students and set student roles.

- You (as administrator) may change student roles at any time on the **Users** tab, **Authors & Users** page.

- Student roles must be set to "Editor" for students to write or create their own page on the class blog.

- Students may set up their own pages within the class blog using the **Write** tab, **Write Page**.

- Have students title their *parent* page as they would a web page or with their user name, rather than their real name.

- Teacher moderates posts/comments on main page and may edit student pages.

- When students write a page that will be a sub-page to their own page, they need to scroll down and specify their own page as the *parent* page.

- Each blog has a theme, or layout design, that determines how the blog will look on the Web. Themes may have one, two, or three columns. Links and pages on the blog may be listed on the left side of the screen or on the right side. There may be tabs across the top of the blog to ease in navigation.

- If students each have their own page, with their work posted on sub-pages, choose the theme carefully—not all themes have active drop down menus or sub-pages listed in a side bar.

- For a theme that lists sub-pages equally with parent pages, have students identify their sub-pages in some way, perhaps with initials before or after the page title or user name then title of specific work.

Sample #2: Class blog with Student pages

http://ottertc.edublogs.org/

Option #3

Students have their own blogs, linked to the main page

- Go to main teacher Gmail account.

- Create filters and labels for students.

- Add students using the **Blog & User Creator** feature Select the **Blog & User Creator** option. This page is self-explanatory for setting up student blogs that will link to your main blog, or home page. You may see a message "error creating blog, blog already exists"—this may refer to the existence of the main class or teacher blog. Wait a minute and then check to make sure that you receive the "Blog created!" message in the message box just below the dashboard.

Student Blogging *(cont.)*

Option #3 *(cont.)*

- Go to **Users** tab **Authors & Users** to set student roles.

- Set student roles to editor, retain your user name as administrator, *before* students log on to their blogs.

- From Administrator **Dashboard** click on **tab** "All my blogs" at the top of the screen. In the "Choose a blog" window, pull down menu to view student blog titles. Click on desired blog to view **dashboard** for that blog.

- Use blogroll to make each page visible to other members of class

Sample #3: Class blog and Student blogs, linked through blog roll

http://ottertc.edublogs.org/

- Each student has his or her own blog

- Teacher has central blog, which students check daily

- Central blog is linked to student blogs

- Class blogroll links to student work

- Teacher may post assignments and resources for students on central blog

- Students share on their blogs

- Teacher may still want to preview student posts as administrator

- Teacher may highlight excellent work samples; drives traffic to student blogs

Option #4

Students have their own blogs, created outside the main class page, but still linked through blogroll

- Use with students age 13 or older

- All pages use edublogs.org platform

- Follow the procedure listed for new users on page 28.

- If students sign in using their own Gmail addresses (separate from teacher's linked Gmail addresses) they will have to activate their own accounts or you will need access to their Gmail accounts.

- Decide whether or not you want to be listed as co-administrator on students' blogs.

- You may wish to use the Student Blog Input form (page 31) and enter all students at one time.

- Students can then manage their blogs.

Sample 4: Class Blog and Individual Student Blogs

http://ottertcr.edublogs.org/

Student User Roles

You (as administrator) are the only one who can access the **Users** tab and change the roles of students. You can set requirements for comment moderation unless students are set as administrators on their own blogs. Students must be added as users to a blog in order to write posts or pages. Otherwise, all they can do on classmates' blogs is comment. When someone views a student webpage from the Internet, they can click on the About page, for example (if listed on template), but there will not be any content unless administrator has made it possible for the student to enter content.

Determine desired student roles and add all students as users on the class blog. A simple form, such as "Student Roles Input Form," on page 38, will assist you or a volunteer in entering information for class user role settings. Students may be set to one role on their own student blogs and a different role on the class blog. For example, you may wish to have older students set as "administrators" on their own personal blogs and as "editors" on the class blog.

Students in any role can access their profiles and change their email addresses and passwords. You cannot access student profiles.

The *administrator* role has access to all blog settings, including:

- add new forums

- add upgrades

- discussion and privacy settings

- access to change blog type (teacher or student)

- edit, add, and delete users

- add users by email address and set user roles

- set up and create student blogs

Think twice before enabling a student user to be an administrator.

Student User Roles *(cont.)*

	Class Blog	Student Blog
Contributor	**Write** posts—submitted for review before posting **Manage** cannot edit or delete posts **Comments** may comment on class blog but may not moderate or manage comments	**Write** posts—submitted for review before posting cannot add links—must be done by administrator **Manage** posts—edit, delete, even prior to review **Comments** cannot approve or delete comments **Settings** cannot access settings page **Profile** can change profile
Author	**Write** posts—without prior review by administrator cannot write pages **Manage** can moderate (edit or delete) own posts but not other posts can search media library **Comments** can view and search comments can moderate (edit or delete) comments **Settings** cannot access settings page **Profile** can access and change profile	**Write** posts—without prior review by administrator cannot write pages **Manage** posts (edit, delete) media library—search **Comments** approve, delete **Settings** cannot access settings page **Profile** can access and change profile

Student User Roles *(cont.)*

	Class Blog	Student Blog
Editor	**Write** post—publish immediately without review, can password protect posts pages links—add new **Manage** posts—can edit and delete posts, even administrator's posts on class blog pages—can edit and delete pages, even administrator's pages on class blog links—edit and delete, change visibility settings categories—add new, edit, or delete tags—add new, edit, or delete search media library **Comments** can approve, edit, and delete comments, including teacher's (administrator) **Settings** cannot access settings page **Profile** can access and change profile settings	**Write** posts immediately without review pages without review links—add new **Manage** posts—edit, delete, even administrator's posts on student blog pages—edit, delete, even administrator's pages on student blog links—can edit or delete categories—add new tags—add new search media library **Comments** can approve, edit, and delete comments, including teacher's (administrator) **Settings** cannot access settings page **Profile** can access profile **Users** cannot add or change users

Checklist for Setting Up Student Blogs

✓ Log in to student blog.

✓ Change password according to "Student Blog Input" form, page 31, or "Planning My Blog," page 39.

✓ Set student roles on class blog and student blog using the "Student Roles Input Form" below.

✓ Check privacy settings.

✓ Change Design and Avatar on student blogs (optional).

✓ Add students as users to classmates' blogs, if desired.

Student Roles Input Form

Student user name	User role on class blog	User role on student blog
Scruffy	*editor*	*administrator*

Planning My Blog

(students)

User Name	
Email address (teacher may complete)	
Password	
URL (teacher will complete)	
Title	
Tagline: what your blog will be about	
Design (teacher may wish to limit themes)	
First work I will publish	
My favorite links (for blogroll)	
Avatar (image—check with teacher)	

Working with Edublogs in the Classroom

Log In

When you first set up a user name, Edublogs will assign a random (letters and numbers) password. Retrieve this password with your login information from the message sent by edublogs to your email address. Make sure that you write down the password and login information!

Go to **www.edublogs.org**. Log in with your user name and password. You will see the Edublogs home screen again with your avatar and a link to **Your dashboard**. Click on the link to access the dashboard for the class blog.

Or, enter the URL in the browser's address bar. The page will redirect to the home page of the blog. To access the dashboard, click **log in**, usually located in the side bar or at the bottom of the template.

Log in tips

☆ *Internet Explorer* or *Firefox* may ask if you want the program to remember your password. Advise students to be sure to select "No" so others cannot use their account once they have left the computer station.

☆ Students should also leave the "remember me" box unchecked in the login window.

☆ Students should always log out when they finish posting to their blog.

Once you log in to your blog, the site will direct you to a dashboard screen, with quick links to work with the blog. Use the tabs on the dashboard to configure the site as you wish. "Edublogs at a Glance," pages 46–51, gives an overview of the features of Edublogs and where to find them from the dashboard. The main features users interact with (writing posts and pages, managing posts, managing comments, design features, and upgrades) are located on the left side of the screen. The tabs for Settings, Plugins, and Users are on the right side of the screen.

Blog Settings

After you log in on your blog's dashboard, go to the **Users** tab and click on **Your profile** to change your password. To change the title and/or tagline for your blog, go to the **Settings** tab on the dashboard and click on **General**. On this screen you may also change the time and date settings and set the preferred language. Use the **Settings** tab to change the **Discussion** and **Privacy** settings as well.

Posts and Pages

Edublogs allows anyone to comment. From the dashboard, go to the **Settings** tab and click on **Discussion** to change the comment moderation settings. The **General** tab under **Settings** has a box to check that requires users to be registered and logged in before they can comment. On the dashboard, go to the **Comments** tab, and click on the **User name** to edit a comment. Click on any desired action to the right of the comment: unapprove, spam (to report a comment as spam), or delete. On this screen you may also search comments by key words.

Working with Edublogs in the Classroom *(cont.)*

〰〰〰〰〰〰〰〰〰〰〰〰〰〰〰〰〰〰〰〰〰〰〰〰〰〰〰〰〰

You will receive email on the master Gmail account when comments on any student blogs need to be moderated, and you will then need to notify students. You can decide not to receive email notification when students comment or when comments are held for moderation, but the notification will still accumulate in your Gmail account. If too many notifications accumulate in your Gmail account and you do not open or delete them, Gmail may close the account. In order to keep the main email account clean and active, you will need to check the **Manage** tab on the dashboard often to moderate posts and comments. If you have another email account, you could use it to receive notifications of student comments. This way, there would be no danger of the Gmail account that you need for linking students to get locked up and you could still moderate student activity on the blog.

You will need to go to the **Users** tab, **Your Profile**, and change your email address to your secondary address. Then go to **Settings** and select the **Discussion** option to send you an email whenever a comment is held for moderation.

On the **Write** post screen, once users have written the content of their posts, they may scroll down the screen for more options. They can add a tag or a category. WordPress offers links to explain more advanced features, such as excerpts, trackbacks, custom fields, and comments & pings. A post may be password protected.

- Caution! A student editor may change the post author to another student's name at the bottom of the post page.

A post made by a student *contributor* will be submitted for review by the administrator. This pending post will appear on the **Manage** posts page of the administrator's dashboard, with a "pending review" status. Students at any user level may post on their own blogs without review. Students may comment on peers' blogs; comments may be subject to moderation.

Write a page refers to compiling a "static" web page, or a page linked to your blog. At the top of the entry screen, users may click on an icon to add media: images, video, audio, or Flash® media files. On any page the author can choose whether or not to add a custom field or to allow comments or pings. Pings let search engines know the blog has been updated. Given that edublogs has comment moderation and the option to limit comments to registered users, which places a safety net in place, allowing pings may help generate traffic to the blog from within the edublogs community.

A page may be password protected. Use the **Page order** feature to place pages in any order on the blog; they need not be chronological. Some themes will display tabs for each page across the header. Administrators and editors may change the page author from the current user to another user name on the blog.

The **Manage** tab has options to edit or delete posts and pages. Links, categories, and tags may be added, edited, sorted, or deleted. Media may also be edited or deleted. You can import posts or comments from another blog system, or export blog information to another blog.

Working with Edublogs in the Classroom *(cont.)*

Administrators can also add and manage a forum. The default setting in Edublogs allows one forum without any upgrades. Once a forum has been added, view the **Forums** page on the **Manage** tab. Select (highlight) the information in the "page code" column, which will have the word "forum:" followed by four numbers. Right-click (or Control-click if you're on a Mac) on the highlighted text and select "Copy." Open a new page on the **Write** tab and in the entry field right-click, then select "Paste" to enter the page code for the forum. In the title line of the page, enter the title for your forum. Visit the site to view the forum. It will appear as a page in the side bar. Once you open the page, you may post in an existing topic or start a new topic. Posts are listed with the most recent post showing at the end of the page. Each person who comments makes a new post; unlike a blog which has posts and comments on a post. A forum is an ongoing discussion.

Use the **Design** tab to change the theme. Not all templates offer easy navigation back to the site administration page (dashboard). In such a case, a click on a link to edit may take you back to the administration screens. Some templates offer editing of the post time stamp. Look for templates (themes) that have a link to Site Admin, RSS feeds, and displays for pages.

Some templates that may work well for blogging with students:

- Connections
- Digg 3 Columns
- Fauna Beta 1
- Fjords04 (four columns may be a little confusing)
- Glorious Day
- Jakarta
- Kubrick
- Mandigo (extremely customizable)
- Misty Look

Edublogs requires credits (purchased) to install **Upgrades**. Browse the tab to find available upgrades. **Plugins** may be activated or deactivated at no cost. Browse the list to find features of interest.

The **Users** tab allows the administrator to add users, change user roles, remove users, invite others to sign up on Edublogs, make changes to his or her profile and avatar, and create student blogs. Student blogs will be visible as tabs along the top of the dashboard, or click on **All my blogs** and click on the arrow to view a pull-down menu. Click on the name of the blog to go to its dashboard.

When you sign students up for a student blog, you should check the ❐ **Yes** box to become co-administrator. Make sure the blog type is set to **Student**. When students log in to their blogs using their own user names, they have all the capabilities of an administrator, including the ability to delete their blogs. *Before students log on to their blogs for the first time, access their blogs as co-administrator and change their user roles.*

Working with Edublogs in the Classroom *(cont.)*

Students logged in to their blogs created using **Blog & User Creator** (with new account information) may access the class home page by clicking on the appropriate tab at the top of the dashboard. If they click on the class home page the site will redirect them to the dashboard for the home page. This dashboard has limited options, depending on the role of the student.

Invite others to view the class blog. Go to **Users** tab **Invites** and click on the link **Click here** to import addresses from Gmail, Hotmail, Lycos, MSN, or Yahoo. You will see a screen where you select your Internet email service, and fields to enter your email address and password. Click on **Continue**.

Change the default message as *desired* to send to people you invite. The default message reads: "Dear _____, *(your email address)* has sent you an invite to sign up at Edublogs.org— **http://edublogs.org**. You can create your account here: **http://edublogs.org/wp-signup.php**. We are looking forward to seeing you on the site." Modify your address list as desired before clicking on Send invites.

Getting Started

- Send parents a permission slip to get approval to set up linked (email) accounts. (See "Parent/ Guardian Permission Form," page 67, for sample.)

- Students will need to learn their logins (email addresses).

- Keep all student log in information (email addresses, passwords) on file. Before students log in for the first time, you may want to use the "Privacy Checklist," page 44, to review the settings for your blog.

Privacy Checklist

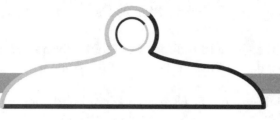

Suggested settings:

Dashboard

Write

Posts

- ✓ allow comments
- ✓ allow pings
- ✓ set password on posts for specific students

Page

- ✓ allow comments
- ✓ allow pings
- ✓ set passwords on pages for specific student groups

Settings

General

- ✓ comment permission—users must be registered and logged in to comment

Discussion

Usual settings for an article:

- ✓ allow people to post comments on the article

Email me whenever:

- ✓ anyone posts a comment
- ✓ a comment is held for moderation

* Gmail may lock the main email account if the class blog(s) have a great amount of comment and post activity, which can cause many emails to be sent to the main (teacher's) email account.

Before a comment appears:

- ✓ an administrator must approve the comment
- ✓ comment author must fill out name and email

Privacy Checklist *(cont.)*

General

   ✓ comment permission—users must be registered and logged in to comment

Discussion

Usual settings for an article:

   ✓ allow people to post comments on the article

Email me whenever:

   ✓ anyone posts a comment

   ✓ a comment is held for moderation

* Gmail may lock the main email account if the class blog(s) have a great amount of comment and post activity, which can cause many emails to be sent to the main email account.

Before a comment appears:

   ✓ an administrator must approve the comment

   ✓ comment author must fill out name and email

   ✓ comment author must have a previously approved comment (optional)

Privacy (teacher preference)

   ❏ I would like my blog to be visible to anyone who visits and in public listings around this site.

   ❏ I would like my blog to be visible to anyone who visits but not appear on public listings around this site.

Blog Type

   ✓ Student

Users

Authors & Users

   ✓ set students to contributor, author, or editor

   ✓ use administrator for teacher only

Blog & User Creator

   ✓ set Blog Type to student

   ✓ set Add Admin to Yes to add yourself (teacher) as co-administrator

Edublogs at a Glance

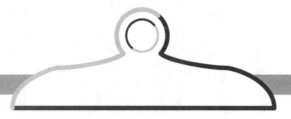

Your blog name

Click Update Options to save changes

Dashboard

Dashboard

quick links to get started

Promote your edublog

may send message about blog to specific email addresses

Widgets

Write

Write Post

Title

Post

- add media

Tags

Categories

Advanced options

- excerpt
- trackbacks
- custom fields
- comments & pings
- password protect post
- post author

Publish status

- option to save and continue editing/writing
- option to keep post private

Edublogs at a Glance *(cont.)*

Write Page

Page title

Page content

- add media

Advanced options

- custom fields
- comments & pings
- password protect page
- page parent
- page template
- page order
- page author

Publish status

- option to save and continue editing/writing
- option to keep page private

Link

Name

Web address

Description

Categories

Advanced options

- target
- link relationship
- advanced

Save

- option to keep link private

Edublogs at a Glance *(cont.)*

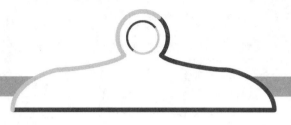

Manage
Posts
>   search posts by key word, date, category, or filter

>   search published posts or drafts

>   edit or delete posts

Pages
>   search pages by key word, or date

>   edit or delete pages

Links
>   search, edit, sort, delete

>   this is the "blogroll"

Categories
>   can add new, edit, search, delete

>   categories can be converted to tags

Tags
>   add new, search, edit, delete

Media Library
>   search, edit, delete

Import
>   import posts or comments from another system

Export
>   saves blog as XML file

>   export to another WordPress-powered blog

Forums
>   add, edit, remove forums depending on upgrade status; default is one forum

Design
Themes
>   choose a theme

Widgets
>   select available widgets to add to the sidebar

Edublogs at a Glance *(cont.)*

Custom Image Header

> visible only with themes that have custom headers
>
> change header image and text color

Comments

Comments

> search, approve, mark as spam, unapprove, delete

Upgrades

> options to accumulate credits to get upgrades

Settings

General

> blog title
>
> tag line
>
> email address
>
> Membership
>
> > ❏ users must be registered and logged in to comment
>
> date and time settings
>
> set language

Writing

> post formatting

Reading

> page displays
>
> syndication feeds

Discussion

> settings for articles
>
> post and comment moderation
>
> comment moderation and spam filters
>
> avatars

Privacy

> blog visibility options on the Web

Edublogs at a Glance *(cont.)*

Miscellaneous

    image sizes

Blog Avatar

    upload picture

Blog Type

    teacher

    student

    other

Dashboard Widgets

    options to edit dashboard

<u>Plugins</u>

    offers variety of plugins to expand functions of WordPress

<u>Users</u>

Authors & Users

    edit, delete, change roles of users

    ✓ subscriber

    ✓ contributor

    ✓ author

    ✓ editor

    ✓ administrator

    search users by user name only

    add user from community—by email address

Your profile

    change display of user name

    change contact information

    add biographical information

    change a password

Your Avatar

    browse and upload new avatar

Edublogs at a Glance *(cont.)*

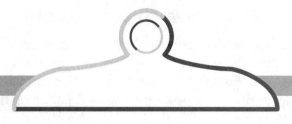

Add Users

    add by email

    set user role

    batches of 15 at a time

    good for adding students created with Gmail links

Invites

    Invite people to sign up at Edublogs

Blog & User Creator

    blog type

    add admin

    blog/user name

    user email

    batches of 15

    can use to set up student blogs

Blogger™ Web Publishing Service

http://www.blogger.com

Blogger remains popular due to the ease of set up and use. The drawback is that Blogger does not allow students under age 13 to "use the service." However, anyone may comment on a blog. Teachers cannot create individual pages, as in Edublogs or Word Press. You can have students post their work as posts, with user names to protect privacy, by using the **Email** function on the Blogger settings page. A student can create content in *Microsoft Word*™, *Excel*™, or *PowerPoint*™ and copy it into an email to send to the blog as a draft. To publish the post, from the blog's **Dashboard**, click on the link for **posts** for that blog. On the **Customize** screen, open the **Posts** tab and click on **Edit Posts**. Click on **Edit** for a particular student's post and preview the draft. If you approve, click on **Publish Posts** at the bottom of the screen. Classmates may then comment on students' work.

Setting Up a Blog

Creating a blog using Blogger takes only a few minutes. The form, "Getting Started with Blogger," page 53, may help in setting up one or more class blogs for your students.

1. Log on to **www.blogger.com** and click on **Create a Blog**.

2. On this same screen Blogger lists the basic steps to creating a blog:

    1) Create an account

    2) Name your blog

    3) Choose a template

3. If you do not have a Google™ Account, Blogger will provide a prompt to create a Google Account.

Google asks for:

- email address (address must already exist)
- password of choice
- display name (user name)
- word verification
- acceptance of terms of service

Google uses this information to set up a free account, which you will use to access Blogger. The user receives notification from Google and Blogger regarding account status and password information, but no spam or junk email.

You will be directed to the next screen.

4. Name your blog. Give the blog a title.

5. Enter the URL you want to use (domain address). The URL will have blogspot.com as part of the address, for example, **http://wcsotter.blogspot.com**. Click on **Check availability**. Change your URL if necessary.

Setting Up a Blog (cont.)

6. Type in word verification.

7. Click on **Continue**.

8. Blogger will redirect to a screen where you can choose a template. Scroll down the center part of the page to see more template options.

9. At this point you should get a message saying "Blog created." You may see a prompt to **view blog**. Click on the link and your blog page will load. Or, click on **Start blogging** to continue. You will see a screen with options to post, change settings or layout, or view the blog.

Getting Started with Blogger

Email address	Password	Display name	Title	URL	Template
lizardgirl33@gmail.com	*sunnyd87*	*lizard girl*	*WCS*	*www.wcsotter.blogspot.com*	*Sample template TCR*

On the home screen, a user may sign in with an existing Google Account by providing email and password. Once you log in with your existing Google Account, Blogger will redirect you to your Dashboard. The screen will display any existing blogs you may already have with Blogger. Towards the top right corner of the dashboard you may click on the **Create a blog** link.

Across the top of the main blog page is the navigation bar. On the right it contains links for **new post**, **customize**, and **sign out**. To the left is a search field to search the blog for a keyword, a link to flag the blog (for objectionable content), and a link to scroll to the next blog. Clicking the Next Blog link takes the reader to the next blog on Blogger's role, regardless of content. Therefore, you might have an interest in disabling the navigation bar so students cannot navigate off the main blog page when they are reading posts and making comments.

Setting Up a Blog *(cont.)*

To disable the navigation bar, view your blog main page. Click on the **customize** link. On the customize screen, click on the **Layout** tab. On this screen, click on **Edit HTML**. With this window still open, open another window in your Internet browser. Go to the link below and follow the instructions, cutting and pasting the code into your **Edit HTML** screen as directed.

http://bloggertricks.com/2007/12/hide-disable-remove-blogger-navbar-from.html

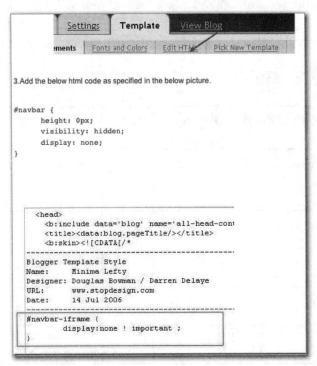

Remember to scroll down to the bottom of the editing screen and click on **Save Template** to save the changes.

Go to **Settings Permissions** and check to make sure you are set up on the blog as an admin. If necessary, add yourself as an author using the email account you plan to use with your Google Account and any blogs you set up. Check your email and click on the link to confirm the invitation. This link will redirect to Blogger and ask you to sign in with your Google Account information. You will be able to view the blog. Click on **Sign out** in the top right corner of the screen.

On the Blogger home page, sign in at the prompt using the blog access user name and password listed above. Go to **Settings Permissions** and grant yourself admin privileges if you have not already done so.

Once you have a blog set up, instruct students to sign on to the blog page using the direct URL link:

http://*nameofblog*.blogspot.com

When viewing the blog, the only thing students can do is comment. To leave the blog, they will have to enter a new URL, for example, the school's website, in the browser's URL bar at the top of the screen. Or, you may want to include links to the school's home webpage and other blogs related to classroom activities on the blog and instruct students to click on links after they have made comments on the blog. Have students use a user name to comment that will be identifiable to classmates but not to the whole world, e.g., initials.

Setting Up a Blog *(cont.)*

Student Blogs

* Blogger has a policy that users under age 13 may not set up a blog. You may choose to set up all blogs under your name and email, using different user names and passwords, and assign the user names and passwords to students. Or, set up a class blog and have students contribute as authors by creating posts and making comments. You may wish to have students create pages using another program, and then link to the student pages within a post or on the blogroll.

Blogger has various attractive features, such as ease of setup, formatting and adding page elements, and setting permissions for reading and writing on the blog. However, in Blogger, one blog equals one page on the Internet. If you want your students to post to a class blog, Blogger works well. If students will have their own pages, they will have to copy or email their work from a separate program. You can use labels to sort student posts.

Use "TCR Student Template" as a template to set up a class blog, which already has the Navigation Bar disabled and privacy settings set.

To access the blog template, first go to the Blogger site:

http://www.blogger.com

Sign in using this account:

    username: *tcrsample@gmail.com*

    password: *blog2640*

URL: **http://tcrstemplate.blogspot.com/**

Setting Up a Blog *(cont.)*

Save the template to your computer:

- Go to **Layout**, then **Edit HTML**.

- Click on **Download Full Template**.

- In the window, select **Save**.

- Select the folder on your computer in which you wish to save the template. Edit the name of the template if desired for ease in identifying it later. Click **Save**.

- When download is complete, **Close** window.

Use "Student Blog Input," page 31, or "Planning My Blog," page 39, to create multiple blogs for classroom use. Volunteers can help with this task. Create the first blog and view the **Customize** screen. On the **Layout** tab, go to **Edit HTML** and place the cursor in the upload template field. Click on **Browse** and navigate to the folder where you saved the template file. Click to **Upload**. You may opt to have students use the template and make appropriate changes as guided by the checklist, "Making This Blog Your Own," page 57. If you decide to set up multiple blogs for classroom use, these blogs can be linked to a "main" class blog page.

The way to set up multiple (student) "web pages," or linked pages, in Blogger is to have a list of links.

1. From the dashboard click on **Layout**. If you have a blog with the navigation bar still enabled, you can view the blog and click on **Customize**.

2. On the **Layout** tab select **Page Elements**.

3. Click on **Add a Page Element**.

4. From the list provided, select **Link List**.

5. Title your list accordingly, e.g., "Ms. Heskett's class." Sorting options include alphabetical order or reverse alphabetical order.

6. Add multiple pages using information from any input form you used to set up the blogs.

   - New site URL—the URL of each blog, or "Blog URL"
   - New Site Name—the name of each blog, or "Blog Title"

7. Click on **Add Link**.

8. When you are done adding links, click **Save**.

9. The user may go back to this screen and **edit** or **delete** links at any time.

Making This Blog Your Own

Go to the **Settings** tab:

<u>Basic</u>

> ✓ check title to make sure it matches your blog
>
> ✓ add a description of your blog if you wish

<u>Publishing</u>

> ✓ check blogspot address to make sure it matches the URL you designated

<u>Comments</u>

enable comment moderation

*For safety reasons it is recommended that you use the teacher's email address here—do not use your own email address!

- **Yes**—Show word verification for comments
- **No**—Show profile image on comments

*Enter teacher's email address here.

<u>Email</u>

BlogSend Address

*you may wish to direct students to insert your email address here for accountability tracking

<u>Permissions</u>

You may wish to determine the desired audience and create the template accordingly. Advise students as to whether or not they may make changes or additions to this screen.

Customizing Your Blog

On the Dashboard, under the "Manage Blogs" heading, you will see links to **Edit Posts**, **Settings**, **Layout** and **View Blog**. From the main blog page, you can access these features using the **Customize** link.

On the customize screen, the **Posting** tab allows the user to **Create** a new post, **Edit posts**, and **Moderate comments**. Any blog author may edit his or her own posts, but not any other posts.

Blog administrators can change the title and description of their blogs, modify various privacy settings, change formatting for posts, set comment moderation and permissions, and make other formatting changes with the **Settings** tab. At the bottom of each screen click on the link to **Save Settings**.

The **Layout** tab allows blog administrators to change the appearance of their blogs.

Settings Overview

Basic

- Title of blog
- Description of blog
- Add your blog to our listings? *no* (will still be on Internet)
- Search engines? *no*
- Quick Editing—up to teacher
- Email post links—probably want *no*
- Global settings—depends on individual
- Compose—*yes*

Scroll to bottom of page to **Save Settings**

Publishing

refers to domain that will host your blog—unless you have a specific domain, use default setting

Formatting

- how many posts on a page
- select posts to show by number of posts or number of days
- format for date, archives, time stamp, time zone, language
- option to link to podcasts

Comments

- option to show or hide comments—to encourage interaction, select show
- Who can comment?
    - ✓ anyone
    - ✓ registered users
    - ✓ users with Google Accounts
    - ✓ only members
- Comments Default for Posts—leave as is
- Backlinks—select *show*

    allows reader to click on link to see all comments in main screen rather than in pop-up window. This is a quick way for teachers to review activity for a specific related post.

- Formatting for comment

    time stamp

    pop-up window

Settings Overview *(cont.)*

- Comment moderation

  ✓ always

    notifies administrator (teacher) when someone leaves a comment—does not always notify for new <u>post</u>

- Word verification

  assures a person, not a machine, is writing on the blog (irrelevant with closed classroom blog)

- Profile images on comments

  good for early in year—allows students to learn screen names or teacher may opt to leave off

Archiving

Set up daily, weekly, or monthly, depending on personal preference

Site Feed

may not be applicable

Email

Use the "mail-to blogger" field to set up a team blog: this allows users to write posts from their email accounts and have it sent to the blog. Teachers may also opt to have posts emailed to them any time someone publishes a post on the blog. Use this function if students will post their work from another program, such as *Microsoft Word*.

Open ID

Allows users to use a single digital (in the form of a URL) code to sign in and access websites

Permissions

Blog Authors

You may want to create a team blog with your 7th and 8th grade students (age 13 or older). A team blog may be created adding several authors. The teacher initially sets up the blog. When new members are added, they may write posts and comments on the blog. Add new authors by listing each email address separately. Invited members will receive an email from "username of blog administrator." The message will contain a link to sign in. They will need a Google Account (may use existing email address; Google accepts Hotmail and Gmail, possibly others). If students need to create new Google Accounts, Gmail is recommended for students and teachers due to the ability to link accounts.

The link students receive via email will redirect them to the dashboard for the class blog. Unless the teacher (blog administrator) grants admin privileges to specific blog authors, students view a dashboard with limited options. They can create posts and edit their own posts. They may also opt to use the email function to post to the blog. They cannot edit or moderate comments. Authors can remove themselves from the blog, but they cannot change any other blog settings. Blog authors do not view the **Layout** tab.

Settings Overview *(cont.)*

Blog Readers

✓ Anybody

✓ Only people I choose

✓ Only blog authors

The blog administrator may allow "anyone" to comment or limit comments to specific user groups. Blog readers can comment on the blog but not post. The settings for who can leave a comment regarding a post on the blog are separate from the settings for authors, who may write a new post to the blog. You will want to moderate comments before they appear on the blog; this allows for an authentic audience of readers yet keeps a net of safety in place. In addition, Blogger may block the blog if too many posts or comments have misspellings or grammatical errors, causing the program to view the blog as spam.

The sample blogs on pages 62–65 give examples of a class blog and student blogs using Blogger.

Safety Checklist for Blogger

Settings:

<u>Basic</u>

     ✓ Add your blog to our listings? **No**

     ✓ Let search engines find your blog? **No**

     ✓ Show email post links? **No** (optional; teacher preference)

<u>Comments</u>

     ✓ Anyone (teacher preference)

     ✓ Enable comment moderation? **Yes**

You may want to enter an email address here to receive notification of comments by nonmembers.

     ✓ Show word verification for comments? **Yes** (reduces spam)

     ✓ Show profile images on comments? **No** (for student privacy)

You may also enter an email address to receive notice when anyone comments on the blog.

<u>Permissions</u>

     ✓ Anybody (teacher preference, depending on purpose of blog)

     ✓ Only people I choose

     ✓ Only blog authors (for example, with a group blog)

Sample Blogs

Sample One: Comment Blog

http://wcseagles.blogspot.com/

- The teacher is the only administrator

- Students comment without being members of the blog.

- Settings must be set so that anyone can comment.

- Teacher writes posts

- Students comment

- To comment on the blog, students will need to have Gmail accounts set up. Students may have their usernames show on their comments, or they may comment as "anonymous," but they will still have to enter their Gmail addresses and passwords on the comment screen. When you moderate comments, you will not be able to edit students' work.

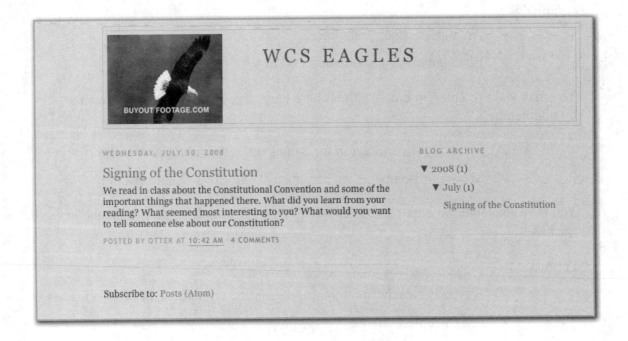

Sample Blogs *(cont.)*

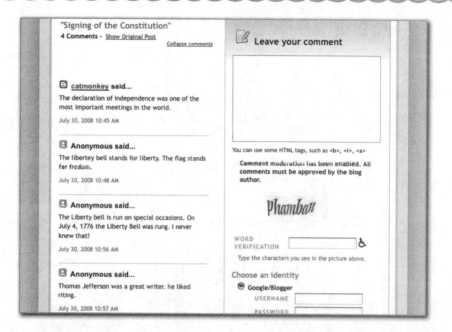

Sample Two: Private Blog

http://wcsotter.blogspot.com/

- The teacher is the only administrator.

- Students comment as contributors. (This sample blog has students listed as authors, but the blog is visible *only* to blog members. It is listed on the Internet as a *"private blog."*)

- Teacher typically posts questions.

- Students reply to questions, which may require research.

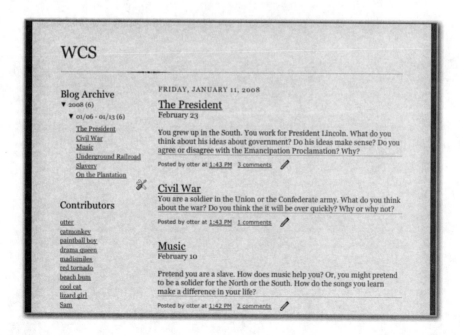

Sample Blogs *(cont.)*

Sample Two: Private Blog *(cont.)*

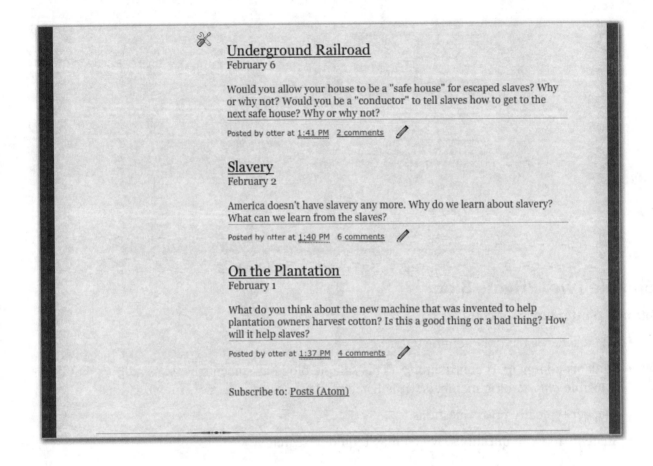

Underground Railroad
February 6

Would you allow your house to be a "safe house" for escaped slaves? Why or why not? Would you be a "conductor" to tell slaves how to get to the next safe house? Why or why not?

Posted by otter at 1:41 PM   2 comments

Slavery
February 2

America doesn't have slavery any more. Why do we learn about slavery? What can we learn from the slaves?

Posted by otter at 1:40 PM   6 comments

On the Plantation
February 1

What do you think about the new machine that was invented to help plantation owners harvest cotton? Is this a good thing or a bad thing? How will it help slaves?

Posted by otter at 1:37 PM   4 comments

Subscribe to: Posts (Atom)

Sample Blogs *(cont.)*

Sample Three: Class Blog

http://otterlearning.blogspot.com/

- Teacher sets up and administrates blog
- Teachers and older students (age 13 and over) participate equally as authors
- Teachers and students make posts and comments
- Teacher structures nature and content of blog

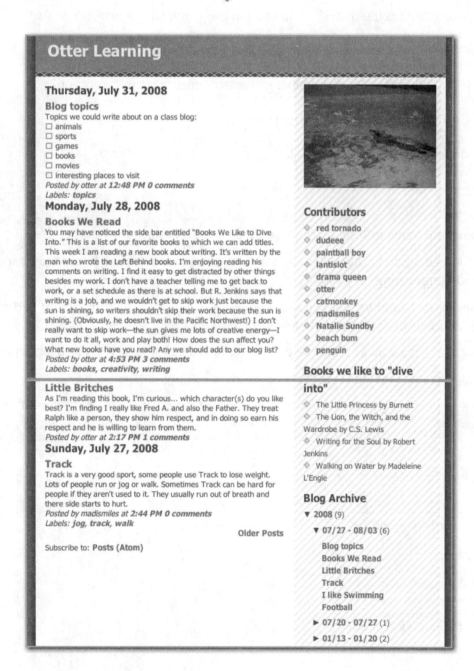

Student Internet Agreement

Rules

✓ Do not edit date stamps on my posts and pages.

✓ Do not edit administrator comments, posts, and pages. *(optional for teacher to use)*

✓ Do not delete administrator comments, posts, and pages. *(optional for teacher to use)*

✓ Do not delete classmates' posts and pages. *(optional for teacher to use)*

✓ Whenever you access the blog site, leave the "remember me" box unchecked.

✓ Always click "no" if the computer asks to remember your password.

✓ Post only original (not copyright) material.

✓ Post only appropriate material.

- I understand and agree to follow school policies and guidelines for Internet use.
- I understand and agree to follow classroom rules and procedures for Internet use, specifically, posting and commenting on a blog.
- I understand that if I fail to follow these guidelines, I will lose the privilege to participate in the class blog and will have to complete alternate assignments.
- I agree not to navigate away from the class blog or student blogs without teacher permission.
- I agree not to change my email address or password in my profile.
- I agree not to post any personal information that might enable strangers to identify me or my classmates.

_____ _____

student signature   *date*

_____

Print student name

Parent/Guardian Permission Form

Dear Parent or Guardian:

With your permission, your child will be participating in a class blog, which may also expose your child to content and access on the Internet at school as part of his or her class instruction. General school rules for behavior and communications apply. The networks are provided for students to conduct research and communicate with others. Access to network services is given to students who agree to act in a considerate and responsible manner. Parent permission is required for independent use. Access is a privilege—not a right. Access entails responsibility.

Below are the rules for use at the school. Please read and discuss these **Internet and Computer Use Guidelines** with your child before you consider granting permission. If you agree, retain a copy of the guidelines on this page for future reference, and return the permission form to your child's teacher. We must have the **Parent/Guardian Permission Form** and **Student Internet Agreement** on file for your child to participate in the classroom blog or access the school computer network.

Guidelines for Internet Usage

1. All students must have a signed permission slip from their parents that authorizes them access to the Internet.

2. Respect for the equipment of the school and its network is a condition for use of the computers.

3. Students are to notify the teacher/librarian immediately of any disturbing material they may encounter on the World Wide Web or in email.

4. Students are not to post personal information such as telephone number, full name, address, email address, or personally identifiable photos on the Internet or give this information to anyone online.

5. Students are to never give anyone their password to any of their accounts or allow another student to use their account to access the Internet or school network.

6. Students must gain clearance from the teacher/librarian before downloading any programs from the Internet.

7. In accordance with student rights and responsibilities, the following are not permitted:

   - Sending or displaying offensive messages or pictures;

   - Using obscene language;

   - Harassing, insulting or attacking (flaming) others;

   - Damaging computers, computer systems or computer network;

   - Violating copyright laws, including software piracy and plagiarism;

   - Using another's password/accounts;

   - Intentionally gaining unauthorized access to network, computer or system directories, resources or entities;

   - Knowingly accessing inappropriate material or delving deeper into inappropriate information accessed accidentally.

Parent/Guardian Permission Form *(cont.)*

I give _____ permission to participate in classroom blog activities. I understand that the blog will be set up in accordance with district Internet use guidelines, and that students must adhere to these guidelines and policies.

As the parent or legal guardian of _____, I have read the Guidelines for Internet Usage and grant permission for my son or daughter or the child in my care to access the Internet. I understand that Internet access is intended for educational purposes only. I also understand that every reasonable precaution has been taken by the school to provide for online safety but the school cannot be held responsible if pupils access unsuitable websites.

❒ **I accept the above paragraph.**   ❒ **I do not accept the above paragraph.**

(Please check the appropriate box.)

I understand that if the teacher considers it appropriate, my child's schoolwork may be chosen for inclusion on the class blog or the school website. I understand and accept the terms of the school relating to publishing children's work on the school website.

❒ **I accept the above paragraph.**   ❒ **I do not accept the above paragraph.**

(Please check the appropriate box.)

Signature: _____   Date: _____

Address: _____   Telephone: _____

_____

Printed Name: _____

Using Blogs in the Classroom

You can group students in different configurations to use blogs in the classroom, such as having students work individually or in a group or blog team. Other examples include contributing to classroom discussion forums or posting their work individually in e-portfolios.

Things to Think About

- ✓ Consider the audience—why someone would visit the blog
- ✓ Establish goals
- ✓ Use a schedule for posting
- ✓ Allow students to vary length of entries
- ✓ Have students write on themes
- ✓ Provide content resources for students
- ✓ Have students use digital cameras and scanners to incorporate graphics and other media into a blog
- ✓ Match the tool (a post on a blog, new page on the blog, *PowerPoint* presentation, video, webpage, Wiki space, etc.) to the project based on the authentic purpose and audience

Ways to Use Blogs in the Classroom

Teachers	Students
post class information	write own blog
post assignments	reflect on what they think about specific topics as they write about those topics
reading material for students	reflective journal
practice exercises	writing journal
link resources that relate to topics of current study	learning log to record new things they have learned
organize/conduct in-class discussions	sharing experiences
content-related blogs to share ideas, tips, etc. with colleagues	assignment review—receiving feedback from teacher as they turn in assignments—a record of incremental progress
networking	dialogue for group work—blogs become a paper trail to keep tabs on who does what
connect content and curriculum to blog technology	E-portfolios of student work
academic subject areas: math, science, social studies, etc.	student newspapers

Using Blogs in the Classroom (cont.)

Ways to Use Blogs in the Classroom (cont.)

Teachers	Students
class discussions	interactive discussions
use password protection feature with pages in Edublogs to work with student groups; or create a private blog in Blogger for a specific student group	writing
give information to students	book discussions/reflections
post relevant resources for classroom activities and assignments	summarize readings
virtual field trips	upload assignments as posts to teacher blog online journals, e.g., on Friday have "read and respond day" when students respond to peers
supplemental / real-world applications	online magazine related to specific topic of interest or current studies
learn with students in other geographic areas	learn with students in other geographic areas
post a quote from Science, Social Studies, or Literature; students respond to quote	writing workshop—students "publish" their work
discussion questions	peer conferencing
upload *PowerPoint* presentation to the blog	upload *PowerPoint* presentation to the blog
Questions & Answers between teacher and students	create specialized glossary or dictionary related to current unit of study
writing lessons	post news or informational articles in response to videos or other media or classroom presentations; journal about process

Sample Lessons

Many students spend great amounts of time on the Internet emailing friends or chatting on MySpace or similar forums. They often use informal language when doing so and write very brief, conversational messages. That is, they may not have experience discussing anything of "substance" in writing outside of school assignments (e.g., reports, essays, etc.).

The following lessons introduce students to concepts of blogging, including vocabulary and response to others by commenting or posting on a blog. They may be used to introduce students to the concept of discussing various topics with someone else using written, rather than oral, language.

You may want to create a list of appropriate blogs and websites that your students will enjoy reading. The "Technology Resources" list (page 92) may give you places to start, or the links listed below may help.

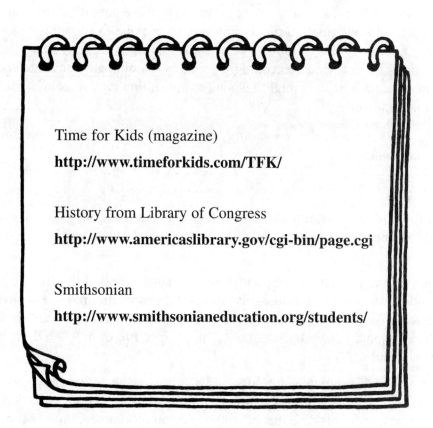

Time for Kids (magazine)

http://www.timeforkids.com/TFK/

History from Library of Congress

http://www.americaslibrary.gov/cgi-bin/page.cgi

Smithsonian

http://www.smithsonianeducation.org/students/

Responding in Community

Objectives

Given sample reading material, students will respond in writing to something they read and respond to peer's comments.

Materials

- "Blogs," pages 74–75, one copy per student
- "Communication System Diagram," page 76, one copy for display
- Sample blog, page 62

Opening

Discuss the concepts of responding to literature and writing to a prompt. Encourage students to "think outside the box"—to think beyond school or work in regard to these activities. Ask students for examples of times when someone might write to a prompt or respond to something they have read. For instance, a parent might remind their child to write a thank you note for a gift they received. Someone might read a short article in a newspaper encouraging readers to nominate a favorite coach for an award. Have students discuss how they might respond to something they read in the school newsletter or newspaper, or on the Internet.

terms: the blogosphere—informally, the community of blogging in which people read blogs and give positive feedback to the authors

Directions

1. Introduce the topic for discussion. Students will read about using blogs in the classroom, particularly the concept of responding to what they read and commenting on someone else's responses.

2. Define and discuss the concept of "respond." When people respond to something, they express feeling or emotion, answer a question, reply to something specific in the text, give a reaction, agree or disagree, express an opinion or a reaction to what they read or hear. Discuss how student responses should be appropriate, polite, and respectful, even when disagreeing or offering constructive criticism.

3. Display a copy of the "Communication System Diagram," page 76, or draw your own diagram. Define and discuss the concept of a "communication system." A communication system is made up of different parts, or in this case, people, who use common procedures to communicate with one another. The system provides a channel for the exchange of information between members of the communication system.

4. Distribute copies of the reading sample, "Blogs," pages 74–75. Have students read the article and write one-paragraph responses to what they read. Encourage students to reflect on prior knowledge and make connections to their own lives as they comment.

5. Students will swap papers with other students. They will read the initial responses their classmates wrote and then write their own comments.

Responding in Community *(cont.)*

6. Have students swap papers again with different classmates. They will read the responses and comment again on either or both responses. Swap once more if time allows.

7. Have students return the papers to the people who first commented on the papers. Once students have their original papers, they should read all the comments. Allow time for students to respond to one or more peer comments on their papers.

Conclusion

Conduct a class discussion on how students participated and provided feedback in a system.

Extension

A. Have students create diagrams to compare a different type of communication system to the communications system exercise they just completed in class.

B. Have students post comments and responses to the class blog to continue the discussion on blogs.

Blogs

(sample article)

A blog is a page on the Internet, a way to publish on the web. Originally, the term "blog" referred to a web log, or a page on which people listed links to various websites and shared them with others, i.e., a log of places they visited on the Internet. Over time, people began to use blogs to write personal comments and reflections and blogs became a form of online journals. In this way blogs provide a place for readers to write down what they think about what they read. Ideally, others will read the blog and write down their reactions to the reflections posted on the blog, resulting in an ongoing conversation. People also use blogs to list, or "log," their favorite blogs or websites of interest. Often a blog will focus on a particular topic or issue. Blogs may contain links to other websites, pictures, lists, videos, or other media content related to the topic. On the Internet, the blog displays entries with the most recent entry first.

Individual people may use blogs to create their own publishing spaces with information, links, and ideas they want to keep for personal reference or to share with others. Blogs also allow a group of people to communicate with each other on one or more specific topics.

On a blog, students can read new information and perspectives, interact and have discussions with other students, teachers, and potentially, others outside the immediate classroom community. Students may use the blog to respond to something they have read or new information they have learned. Students might gather information and research a particular topic to share on the blog. Peers and others may respond to their comments, resulting in a conversation in which participants learn from each other.

As students post and comment on a blog, others read what they have written. Automatically, their writing now has an authentic audience. Students respond to their peers' writings, evaluating and commenting on the writings.

Students might post assignments, personal reflections, opinions, and comments on material posted on the blog or outside information.

Blogs *(cont.)*

A classroom blog provides students with the opportunity to form an interactive community. As students read others' thoughts, they might begin to change their own thinking as they respond to new ideas. Blogs also provide students with opportunities to become "experts" on topics and share their knowledge with others.

Blogs allow everyone to participate, regardless of ability. Quieter students may feel more comfortable communicating with peers using the written word. Everyone has equal opportunity to express themselves, even if some people say more in class.

Communication System Diagram

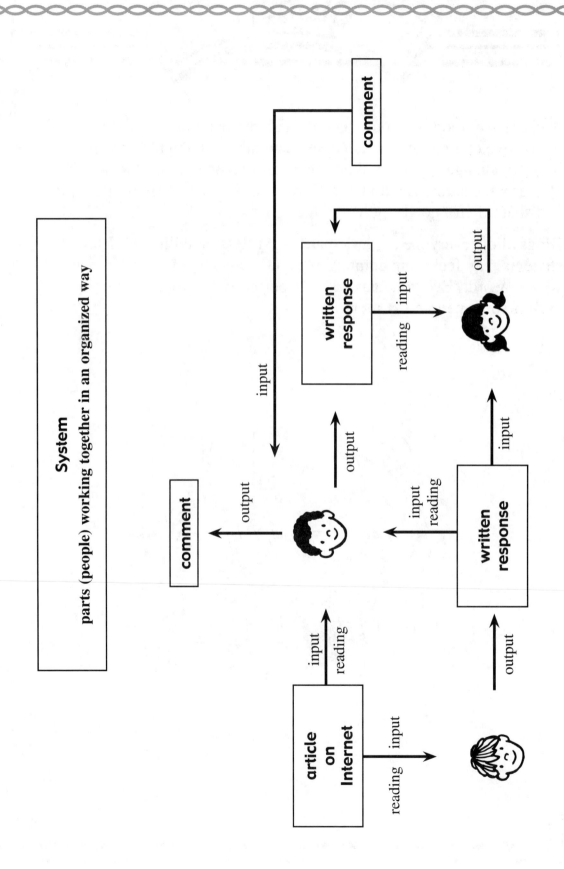

Interact with Reading

Objectives

Given the opportunity to read a variety of material, students will respond appropriately by writing a reflective paragraph and commenting on classmates' writing.

Materials

- Sample blogs or Internet articles
- Sample trade books or print magazines
- Other reading material relevant to students or current topics of study
- Sticky notes or note cards, two or three per student

Preparation

You may want to search blogs on specific topics and provide links (blogroll) for students to access those particular blogs to read and respond. Or, provide articles on various subjects for students to read.

Sample blogs:

Weather, clouds **http://www.eo.ucar.edu/kids/sky/clouds1.htm**

Social Studies **http://ljones2teach.edublogs.org/category/social-studies/**

Opening

Discuss with students how blogs allow them to interact with content material as well as other students' work. They can use their background knowledge and preconceptions to respond to new ideas, comment on posts, and make connections with academic topics of current study.

Directions

1. Generate a class list of media to which students can respond by writing on a blog. Although the primary focus of this lesson is reading, encourage students to think of other media forms as well. A sample list might include: recent news events, live performances (concerts, plays, other live events), songs, movies, books, newspaper articles, something on TV, etc.

2. Focus students' attention specifically on responding to what they read. Review with students some purposes for reading: to understand a topic or issue, to interpret the author's viewpoint, for entertainment, to solve a problem, to answer a specific question, to form an opinion, to gather facts.

3. Model for students how to write a reflective paragraph, expressing new information they learned, new ideas they thought of, and their opinions of what the author said.

4. Have students select one of the sample texts to read. They will write two or three paragraphs to respond to what they read. Remind students to reflect on what they learn.

Interact with Reading *(cont.)*

Closing

Have students post their reflective writing on the class blog. If a blog has not yet been set up, post student writing on a bulletin board. Students may comment on peers' writing using sticky notes or note cards as time allows to practice commenting and posting. Remind students to comment appropriately as discussed in "Responding in Community" (pages 72–73).

Extension

Have students write papers on topics about which they are "experts." Encourage them to consider their audience (who will be responding to students' writing) as they write. They may then share their papers with another class or post on the class blog to generate comments from readers outside the classroom.

Blogging with Your Family

Objective

Given the opportunity to explore Internet safety issues within the confines of the classroom environment, students will demonstrate their understanding of and willingness to comply with acceptable use policies at home or the school library by working with a group to create a portion of a class presentation on safe blogging and by sharing the information with family members.

Materials

- "Student Internet Agreement," page 66, one copy per student and one copy for display as needed
- "Parent/Guardian Permission Form," page 67, one copy per student and one copy for display as needed
- Articles on "safe" blogging, for example:

Microsoft

http://www.microsoft.com/protect/family/activities/blogging.mspx

Math Musings by a middle school teacher

http://mathmusings.blogspot.com/2006/01/safe-blogging.html

Australia's Net Alert

http://www.netalert.gov.au/advice/services/blogs/How_can_children_stay_safe_using_blogs.html

- Access to *PowerPoint* software or cardstock, colored pencils, markers

Preparation

* **Note:** Students may not have Internet access at home or family members who would be willing or able to participate in such a family activity. Students may wish to consider blogging only within the school environment or with other relatives or trusted friends.

Teacher may need to assist students as they compile the PowerPoint presentation for the class.

Opening

Ask students in what ways they try to stay safe. What are some safe practices they follow in their everyday lives? How might those practices apply to using computers, specifically commenting or posting on a blog?

Directions

1. Have students complete a quick-write on what they perceive to be the safety and privacy issues with blogging outside the classroom.
2. Students will then research and read articles and become "experts" on safe blogging.

Blogging with Your Family *(cont.)*

3. Conduct a class discussion to summarize students' research as well as their prior knowledge.

4. Review safe blogging:

   - Do not post an identifiable picture of yourself. A group photo, such as a family photo, in which specific family members are not named, would be ok.

   - Do not put personal information on the blog that would make it easy for a stranger to identify you, such as name, address, age, birthday, last names of friends or relatives, general location, school, phone number, email contact, etc.

5. Have students work with small groups to compile their responses into one slide for a class *PowerPoint* presentation. If students do not have access to computers, they may create their "slides" using cardstock and markers.

6. Create the *PowerPoint* presentation.

7. Show the presentation to others at a school assembly if possible.

Closing

Review the Student Internet Agreement (page 66) and Parent/Guardian Permission Form, including the Guidelines for Internet Usage (pages 67–68) with students. Discuss the reasons for these guidelines as a class. Have students sign copies of the Student Agreement if they have not already done so and send copies of both forms home with students to obtain parent signatures.

Have students create a safety manual brochure to take home and share with their families about how to safely participate in a family blog.

Extension

Students may roleplay safe and unsafe blogging practices.

Learning the Language

<<<<<<<<<<<<<<<<<<<<<<<<<<<<<<<<<<<<<<<<<<<<<<<<<<<<<<

Objective

Given an introduction to blogging terms and reference materials, students will learn the meanings of terms and create illustrated dictionaries or glossaries.

Materials

- "Blog Terminology," pages 20–21, one copy for teacher reference, one copy for display as needed
- Index cards
- World maps
- Foreign dictionaries or access to Internet
- White construction paper, 9" x 12" (23 cm x 30 cm), one piece per student
- Colored pencils, crayons, markers
- Access to *Microsoft Word*, *Microsoft PowerPoint*, *Microsoft Publisher*, or other desktop publishing software (optional)
- Dictionary, thesaurus (optional)
- Access to online dictionary, thesaurus (optional)
- Globe (optional)

Preparation

Use index cards and the list of terms on "Blog Terminology," pages 20–21, to prepare word cards, with one word on each card. Prepare a second set of cards with one definition on each card. Display the world maps around the classroom and post word cards with the maps. Do not post the definition cards.

Gather foreign words for common terms such as "hello," "good-bye," "computer," etc.

Opening

Share with students different ways people say "hello," "good-bye," "computer," and a few other common terms around the world. Ask students which terms they could understand without knowing how to speak the language. Explain that some fields of study have a common language, for example— many medical terms are from Greek or Latin, many legal terms come from Latin, and much of the terminology they will learn about blogging originated in English, as the majority of the Internet structure originated in the United States.

Directions

1. Ask students how they would define the term "blog-o-sphere." Direct students' attention to the map and word card displays. Explain that each student will receive a definition card. He or she will find the word that their card defines posted somewhere around the room. Students may use dictionaries as necessary.

2. Students will work in groups after they have matched the word cards and definitions. You may wish to have them find their word cards in groups if that works better logistically.

Learning the Language *(cont.)*

3. Once students have matched their definition cards with the correct word cards, have them work in their groups.

4. Groups will create glossary pages to define and illustrate their terms.

Closing

Have students share their pages with other members of the class. Bind the pages to create a class Blogging dictionary; you may want to make more than one copy for classroom use or to share with another class.

Extension

A. Have students use the word and definition cards to quiz each other on blog terminology, playing a game similar to "Go Fish."

B. Students may use desktop publishing software to create their glossary pages, if desired.

Designing a Blog

Objectives

Given exposure to sample blogs, students will design an effective blog as determined by the traffic their blog receives.

Materials

- Sample blogs (copies of pages 62–65 or screen shots of teacher's favorite blogs)
- White cardstock, 8 ½" x 11" (22 cm x 28 cm), one piece per student
- Markers, colored pencils, or crayons
- Sticky notes, several per student

Opening

Ask students to describe blogs they have viewed on the Internet. Have them explain what they liked about the blogs and what caught their attention.

Directions

1. Distribute cardstock to students and have other supplies available for student use. Have students design the "home pages" of their blogs. Encourage them to choose "user names," since their "blogs" will be displayed anonymously.

2. Encourage students to write short articles that would display on their home pages, such as welcome posts, or a post describing what the blog will be about.

3. Display student blogs around the room. Give each student a few sticky notes. Have students visit the sites of their choice, making comments on each blog using sticky notes. Students should sign their comments with their usernames.

Conclusion

Discuss which blogs received the most traffic and what made those blogs attractive to students, e.g., color, layout, design, lettering, etc.

Extension

Have students give one or two positive comments as well as suggestions for improvement for two blogs they did not visit.

How to Respond on a Blog

Objective

Given reading material in content areas, students will respond to what they read and post on the class blog.

Materials

- Sample reading material in relevant content area, e.g., textbooks, library books, magazines, Internet articles (or specific links), etc.

- Selected article for students, one copy per student

- URL for class blog

Preparation

Select one brief article for all of the students to read. Set up a class blog and any student email accounts or passwords necessary for students to access the blog.

Opening

Refer to prior lesson, "Responding in Community" (pages 72–73), if applicable. Review with students the concept of how to "respond." Discuss with students different language structures they use to respond in various situations, such as using informal language when talking with friends in person or writing a letter, formal language when writing a report for school, or very informal language in an email. Remind students that anything they write in a post or a comment on a blog will have a public audience beyond the classroom. They will need to write in such a way that their readers will be able to understand the writing.

Directions

1. Have students volunteer suggestions of what they might include in a response: they can agree, disagree, share their thoughts and insights, make connections, ask questions, and give feedback as they would in a conversation.

2. They might write about the same things they would when they respond to literature, or when they discuss topics orally with a small group or in class for various academic subjects (e.g., Social Studies).

3. Distribute copies of the selected article. Have them read the article and respond verbally in small groups to what they read. You may wish to do this step as a whole group and model a response for the students.

4. Students may then respond to the article by writing letters to someone in the class. Classmates will then respond to the letters in writing.

5. Students will respond by commenting on the responses their classmates wrote to the original letters. Review the concept of responding to a prompt (see lesson "Responding in Community," pages 72–73).

How to Respond on a Blog *(cont.)*

Closing

Have students post their original responses to reading on the class blog.

Extension

A. Have students take copies of the selected article home as well as their written responses to the article. Students can ask family members to read the article and comment on the students' responses, with the student then responding to the family member.

B. Students may read other sample reading materials in content areas and respond to what they read by posting or commenting on the class blog. Remind students to include something that identifies what article they read in the subject line of their post.

How to Post on a Blog

Objective

Given a quote from literature, students will make connections and practice posting on the class blog.

Materials

- Display copy of **http://ottertcr.edublogs.org/writing-about-wild-animals/**
- Textbook with glossary, e.g., Social Studies or Science (optional)
- Chart paper, colored markers
- Plain white paper, 8 ½" x 11" (21.5 cm x 28 cm), one piece per student
- URL to class blog

Preparation

Access the link listed above. Display the site on a classroom monitor, or print out a copy of the article for student use. Set up any needed student accounts and page(s) for the class blog.

Opening

Ask students to describe what they know about writing a post on a blog. What features attract someone to read a post? What makes the post easy or hard to read? What is a hyperlink and why would you include it in a post?

Directions

1. Display or distribute the article on writing a post. Read through the article together.

2. If students need further explanation to understand the concept of a hyperlink, demonstrate by showing them a page of a textbook that has a highlighted glossary word. Ask students what they might do when they read that word on the page. (*They could turn to the glossary at the back of the book to learn more about what the word means.*) In the same way, a page on the Internet might have a highlighted or underlined word. The reader can click on that word to go to a link on the Web to find out more about that topic. If students view the article online, demonstrate by clicking on the link in the article.

3. Discuss the questions in the article.

4. Brainstorm with students ideas for topics they might write about on the class blog. Use chart paper and markers to create a class list of possible topics.

5. Have students use a blank piece of paper to generate an idea web to write a post about one of the topics. Remind students that their posts will not need to be too long, and they will need titles for their posts. Encourage them to incorporate one or more of the features discussed in the article.

6. Students should write a draft of their post before entering it on the class blog.

How to Post on a Blog *(cont.)*

Closing

Have students post their writing on the class blog. Invite students to read and comment on their classmates' posts. Have them share what they learned and what they enjoyed about reading other people's work.

Extension

Have students read one or more posts from approved blog listings. Students may then share with the class about something they read, or something new they learned. Have them also tell what they learned about writing effective posts from reading blogs.

On the Road to Responsible Blogging

Objective

Given guidelines, students will create posters for the class computer area; students will read sample posts and evaluate them according to class guidelines.

Materials

- White cardstock, 8 ½" x 11" (21.5 cm x 28 cm), one piece per student
- Markers, colored pencils, crayons
- Sample road signs: **http://www.trafficsign.us/**
- Sample blog posts: **http://sampletcr.blogspot.com/**
- "Sample Blog Screenshots," pages 90–91 (optional)

Opening

Display road signs, either from Internet sites or library resource materials. Ask students what type of information or messages these signs convey to readers (rules, warnings, markers, guides; get drivers' attention, give adequate time for proper response, e.g., turning a corner). Compare responsible blogging to responsible driving (or bicycle riding). Discuss what similar information students would need to act responsibly.

Directions

1. Display sample blog posts or distribute copies of "Sample Blog Screenshots," pages 90–91. Have students read sample blog posts. Ask them to identify responsible and irresponsible writing, or blog behavior. Which posts do not follow the example guidelines below?

   (*"New Learning" does not follow A; "Learning about Links" does not follow B, C, D; "About Me" (Profile) does not follow E, G; "My Friend," does not follow F, I; "Gardens" does not follow J, L, M.*)

2. Continue the discussion about blogging responsibly, based on what students have already learned and experienced with blogs.

3. Have students create road signs for the computer area of the classroom. Examples might include:

   A. Use quotation marks when you refer to something someone else said or wrote.

   B. Acknowledge sources.

   C. Link to websites that gave you ideas.

   D. If you write about someone else's blog or Web page, link to it, and also tell the person. They will probably want to hear how you remembered their site.

   E. Set boundaries—Be Aware.

   F. Watch what you say about other people.

On the Road to Responsible Blogging *(cont.)*

G. Watch how much you say about yourself.

H. Watch your tone when you write—be respectful and courteous.

I. Proofread what you write and make sure it does not offend anyone.

J. Use proper spelling and grammar.

K. Remember you have a world-wide audience.

L. Stay on topic.

M. Include your user name on your posts so your classmates will know you wrote that great piece.

Closing

Display student posters in classroom computer area. Acknowledge students as they blog responsibly on the class blog.

Extension

Have students participate in a panel discussion about what they can do to be more responsible on blogs and the Internet. You might form three or four panels of students and assign each panel a different subtopic. Panels can research and discuss their topic, then present a panel discussion before the class. Students and teachers can generate questions for the panel(s) to answer.

Sample Blog Screenshots

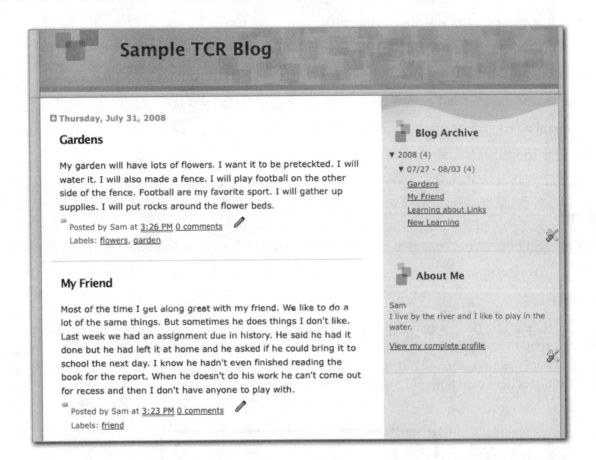

Sample TCR Blog

◘ **Thursday, July 31, 2008**

Gardens

My garden will have lots of flowers. I want it to be preteckted. I will water it. I will also made a fence. I will play football on the other side of the fence. Football are my favorite sport. I will gather up supplies. I will put rocks around the flower beds.

Posted by Sam at 3:26 PM 0 comments
Labels: flowers, garden

My Friend

Most of the time I get along great with my friend. We like to do a lot of the same things. But sometimes he does things I don't like. Last week we had an assignment due in history. He said he had it done but he had left it at home and he asked if he could bring it to school the next day. I know he hadn't even finished reading the book for the report. When he doesn't do his work he can't come out for recess and then I don't have anyone to play with.

Posted by Sam at 3:23 PM 0 comments
Labels: friend

Blog Archive

▼ 2008 (4)
  ▼ 07/27 - 08/03 (4)
    Gardens
    My Friend
    Learning about Links
    New Learning

About Me

Sam
I live by the river and I like to play in the water.

View my complete profile

Learning about Links

When I am researching on the Web, I often come across very interesting sites. It's hard to remember what I found where. One of the things we can do with a blog is to keep track of those sites, often with a Link list, or Blog roll. I'm not going to set one up now, I'll just tell you about a couple of interesting blogs I found.

If you like dragons and fantasy, you might want to look at this blog.

http://dragonbloggin.blogspot.com/

Another blog I like to look at now and then is the miniLegends 08. Next school year the number at the end might change, I'm not sure.

What are some of your favorite blogs?

Posted by Sam at 3:04 PM 0 comments
Labels: blogs, link

Sample Blog Screenshots *(cont.)*

What are some of your favorite blogs?

 Posted by Sam at 3:04 PM 0 comments

Labels: blogs, link

New Learning

"It's what you learn after you know it all that counts." Harry Truman

What do you think this quote means? How can thinking about what you already know help you understand something new?

You learn something every day if you pay attention. Ray LeBlond

Do you think the second quote is true? Why or why not? What have you learned today?

 Posted by Sam at 2:53 PM 0 comments

Subscribe to: Posts (Atom)

Technology Resources

2 Cents Worth

http://davidwarlick.com/2cents/

More information for teachers on education and technology

10 Habits of Successful Bloggers

http://coolcatteacher.blogspot.com/2006/03/ten-habits-of-bloggers-that-win.html

Academy of Discovery

http://academyofdiscovery.com/wp/

http://academyofdiscovery.wikispaces.com/

Site with sample student blogs and other Web 2.0 information

Blogs in Education

http://awd.cl.uh.edu/blog/

Resources for using blogs with students

Bootstrapper

http://www.terrylinks.com/BBT

Links to research different blog platforms and articles on how to design a blog

Class Blog Meister

www.classblogmeister.com

Site that hosts teacher and student blogs. Must register school with webmaster to participate.

Classroom 20

http://www.classroom20.com/

Web site with resources and links on using technology in the classroom

Creating LifeLong Learners

http://www.needleworkspictures.com/ocr/blog/

K-5 teacher's blog on technology in education

Davis, V.

http://coolcatteacher.blogspot.com/2006/08/how-to-comment-like-king-or-queen.html

Sample teacher blog with tips for teaching students to blog

Technology Resources *(cont.)*

Edublogger

http://feeds.technorati.com/blogs/theedublogger.edublogs.org?posts

tips and information for teachers using edublogs in the classroom

Edublogs

http://theedublogger.edublogs.org/2008/02/13/tips-on-blogging-with-students/

Edublogs' tips for teachers contains links to helpful documents

Education World

http://www.educationworld.com/a curr/voice/voice123.shtml

Dyck, B. (2004, May 3). Log On to a Blog. [website article]. *Education World*. Retrieved July 14, 2008.

This article gives an example of blogging in the classroom, as well as guidelines for assessing student work on blogs.

Education World

http://www.educationworld.com/a tech/tech/tech217.shtml

Jackson, L. (2005). Blogging? It's Elementary, My Dear Watson! [website article]. *Education World*. Retrieved July 14, 2008.

This article gives an overview to blogging in the elementary school clssroom and lists various web platforms teachers may use. The article also includes links for a blogging rubric, safety tips, etc.

eMints National Center

http://www.emints.org/ethemes/resources/S00000694.shtml

Sites to help teachers and students design websites

Google

http://www.googlepagecreator.com

Offers another way for teachers and students to post web pages with nothing more than a Gmail account

Google Page Creator is a **Google Labs** project, and is still in an early testing phase. **(https://www.google.com/accounts/ServiceLogin?service=pages&continue=http%3A%2F%2Fpages.google.com%2F&ltmpl=yessignups)**

International Society for Technology in Education

http://www.iste.org/

Includes resources and support for teachers in educational technology

Technology Resources (cont.)

Internet Search Engine Directory

http://www.searchengineguide.com/searchengines.html

search engines grouped by category

Mahara

www.mahara.org

Open Source program for managing e-portfolios

Moving at the Speed of Creativity

Wesley Fryer

http://www.speedofcreativity.org/

Resources for teachers: technology in education

Pair-a-Dimes for Your Thoughts

http://pairadimes.davidtruss.com/

blog about education and technology

Photoshop Support

http://www.photoshopsupport.com/tutorials/jennifer/blog-templates.html

links to free blog templates, information on RSS feeds, tutorials, and more

ProBlogger

http://www.problogger.net/

ProBlogger Tips for Beginning Bloggers

http://www.problogger.net/archives/2006/02/14/blogging-for-beginners-2/

Support Blogging

www.supportblogging.com

Resources and links to education blogs. Click on List of Bloggers in left side bar to see links to classroom blogs by teachers

techLEARNING

www.techlearning.com

Technology resources for teachers and others in education

Technology Resources (cont.)

Technorati

http://www.technorati.com/

Offers a directory of blogs by subject. Teachers may browse to find blogs to link to topics of current study. Not sorted within category, user just has to browse.

Web Node

http://www.webnode.com/en/

free software to host web page

may use your own existing domain

Weblogged

http://weblogged.wikispaces.com/New+Internet+Literacies

Introduction to role of Internet in education, with links to various technology resources

Webopedia

http://www.webopedia.com/

Online dictionary of computer and Internet terms

Wiki spaces

http://www.wikispaces.com/

Allows ad-free wiki for educators

Bibliography

Cowan, J. (2008, June). diary of a blog: listening to kids in an elementary school library. [Electronic version]. *Teacher Librarian*, 35. Retrieved July 14, 2008, from Proquest database http://proquest.umi.com.ezproxy.apollolibrary.com/pqdweb?index=0&did=1502965271&SrchMode= 1&sid=6&Fmt=3&VInst=PROD&VType=PQD&RQT=309&VName=PQD&TS=1216061756&client Id=13118

Downes, S. (2004, September/October). Educational Blogging. *Educause Review, 39.* (5) 14-26. Retrieved December, 2007, from http://connect.educause.edu/Library/EDUCAUSE+Review/ EducationalBlogging/40493

Magid, L. (2006, January 15). Helping Your Kids Blog Safely. [Electronic article]. CBS News. Retrieved July 18, 2008, from http://www.cbsnews.com/stories/2006/01/15/scitech/pcanswer/ main1209925.shtml

Richardson, W. (2004, April 27). Metablognition. *Weblogg-Ed.* Retrieved May 16, 2008, from http://www.weblogg-ed.com/2004/04/27

Rowse. D. (2006, February 18). Writing Good Content. [Web post]. Retrieved July 10, 2008, from http://www.problogger.net/archives/2006/02/18/writing-good-content/

Rowse, D. (2006, October 12). 10 Techniques to Get More Comments on Your Blog. [Web post]. Retrieved July 11, 2008, from http://www.problogger.net/archives/2006/10/12/10-techniques-to-get-more-comments-on-your-blog/

Rowse, D. (2006, February 210. More on Writing Content for Your Blog. [Web post]. Retrieved July 11, 2008, from http://www.problogger.net/archives/2006/02/21/more-on-writing-content-for-your-blog/

Rowse, D. (2004, September 23). Set Boundaries. [Web post] Retrieved July 11, 2008, from http://www.problogger.net/archives/2004/09/23/set-boundaries/?jal_no_js=true&poll_id=12

Shaw, Rosemary. "Teaching Students How to do Online Research." tech-Learning: The Resource of Education Technology Leaders. July 1, 2003.